YORK NOTES

THE
IMPORTANCE
OF BEING
EARNEST

OSCAR WILDE

NOTES BY RUTH ROBBINS

 Longman

The right of Ruth Robbins to be identified as Author of this
Work has been asserted by her in accordance with the
Copyright, Designs and Patents Act 1988

YORK PRESS
322 Old Brompton Road, London SW5 9JH

PEARSON EDUCATION LIMITED
Edinburgh Gate, Harlow,
Essex CM20 2JE, United Kingdom
Associated companies, branches and representatives throughout the world

First published 1999
This new and fully revised edition first published 2005

ISBN 1–405–80173–5

Typeset by Pantek Arts Ltd, Maidstone, Kent
Colour reproduction and film output by Spectrum Colour
Produced by Pearson Education Asia Limited, Hong Kong

CONTENTS

PART ONE

INTRODUCTION

HOW TO STUDY A PLAY

Studying on your own requires self-discipline and a carefully thought-out work plan in order to be effective.

- Drama is a special kind of writing (the technical term is 'genre') because it needs a performance in the theatre to arrive at a full interpretation of its meaning. Try to imagine that you are a member of the audience when reading the play. Think about how it could be presented on the stage, not just about the words on the page.

- Drama is always about conflict of some sort (which may be below the surface). Identify the conflicts in the play and you will be close to identifying the large ideas or themes which bind all the parts together.

- Make careful notes on themes, character, plot and any sub-plots of the play.

- Why do you like or dislike the characters in the play? How do your feelings towards them develop and change?

- Playwrights find non-realistic ways of allowing an audience to see into the minds and motives of their characters, for example soliloquy, aside or music. Consider how such dramatic devices are used in the play you are studying.

- Think of the playwright writing the play. Why were these particular arrangements of events, characters and speeches chosen?

- Cite exact sources for all quotations, whether from the text itself or from critical commentaries. Wherever possible find your own examples from the play to back up your opinions.

- Always express your ideas in your own words.

These York Notes offer an introduction to *The Importance of Being Earnest* and cannot substitute for close reading of the text and the study of secondary sources.

> **QUESTION**
> Discuss the ways in which *The Importance of Being Earnest* both uses and subverts the conventional associations of the 'stock' characters of the comedy of manners.

READING *THE IMPORTANCE OF BEING EARNEST*

Oscar Wilde's play *The Importance of Being Earnest* was premiered in London, at the St James's Theatre on 14 February 1895, and it opened to rave reviews. The critic William Archer, writing in *World* magazine on 20 February, for example, wrote:

> It is delightful to see, it sends wave after wave of laughter curling and foaming round the theatre; but as a text for criticism it is barren and delusive. It is like a mirage oasis in the desert, grateful and comforting to the weary eye – but when you come close up to it, behold! it is intangible, it eludes your grasp. What can a poor critic do with a play which raises no principle, whether of art or morals, creates its own canons and conventions, and is nothing but an absolutely wilful expression of an irrepressibly witty personality? (Quoted in Karl Beckson, ed., *Oscar Wilde: The Critical Heritage*, pp. 189–90)

Those few remarks tell us a great deal about the play. Its appeal comes first of all from its comedy. It is full of brilliant jokes – verbal **repartee**, visual jokes (**sight gags**) and **stage business** – which have remained fresh and funny for more than a hundred years. The jokes remain funny, we must assume, because they express anxieties that remain current today, in particular, the question of sexual comedy: the questions of how the sexes respond to each other, of how men and women should behave, of what the proper roles of gender might be are still problematic, and therefore remain the source of sometimes anxious laughter even today.But the play also appealed to William Archer because it was so very different from the ordinary fare of the London West End of the 1890s.

It is the difference of the play from what was usually to be expected that made it popular at the time; and its continued popularity draws on the very features about which Archer almost complains, namely its elusiveness, its lack of 'principle' or overt **moral**, and its wit.Archer's comments, that is, suggest that this is a play that it is all but impossible to analyse or criticise.

His expectation, as a late-nineteenth-century critic, is that plays are about moral problems and conflicts. Without such features, there is

**CHECK
THE BOOK**

In *Oscar Wilde and the Theatre of the 1890s*, Kerry Powell suggests, on the contrary, that the play derived its original effects from the extensive use it makes of the conventions of the contemporary (1890s) stage. He shows the extent to which Wilde borrowed plot elements, jokes and situations from other plays on the stage at the time, and he argues throughout his book that Wilde's writing is extensively dependent on conventions and plots that were current on the stage of the 1890s.

nothing for the critic to say, except to note his personal responses of amusement and pleasure to the material that Oscar Wilde presented. In fact, it is precisely that the play refuses to talk seriously about moral problems, or to represent its actions realistically, which explains its continued appeal. Oscar Wilde's dramatic method, although it arises out of the realistic or naturalistic tradition of Victorian drama and draws also on the popular forms of melodrama and farce, predicts some of the developments of twentieth-century modernist drama. In particular, the concentration on speeches rather than deeds, static spectacle rather than dynamic action, and on forms of characterisation that belie the ideas of individuality and uniqueness, all align *The Importance of Being Earnest* to developments in drama from Beckett to Pinter, whose works also experiment with minimal plots and characterisation and whose meanings are at least as much in what is not said as what is openly stated or overtly presented.

CHECK THE BOOK

See the Introduction to Ruth Robbins, *Pater to Forster, 1873–1924* for a discussion of the main principles of Victorian criticism.

However, to see the play as an avant garde drama would seem perverse or obscure to many readers and spectators. *The Importance of Being Earnest* is a sure-fire winner in the West End, for touring professional companies, and, indeed, for productions by amateur dramatics societies and schools. Neither the audiences nor the players in these contexts are noted for their openness to experimental drama. Indeed, they are presumed to prefer the safe and the tame. One of the remarkable things about *Earnest*, then, is its commercial success with relatively conservative audiences whilst at the same time, it is also a play which mocks the very conventions that these audiences are supposed to enjoy. It is the complexity of the relationships between the staged spectacle and the audience which observes it that makes the play so special. It treads a series of tightropes: between experimental drama and commercial success; convention and subversion; propriety and outrageousness; it makes us laugh, but it can also be staged as a play with the potential to shock us. Broadly speaking, the play belongs to the genre of the comedy of manners.

CHECK THE BOOK

Katharine Worth makes the suggestion that *Earnest* can be best understood as an experimental drama in her book *Modern Dramatists: Oscar Wilde*.

The term 'comedy', perhaps self-evidently, refers to a play whose primary purpose is to entertain its audience, to amuse them, and which presents a happy resolution of the plot for all the characters with whom the audience sympathises. A good supplementary

CHECK THE BOOK
Kerry Powell, in *Oscar Wilde and the Theatre of the 1890s*, suggests, alternatively, that best generic classification for the play is farce.

definition of comedy is offered by a character from *The Importance of Being Earnest*, Miss Prism, the governess, who has written a novel. Its plot is a comic one because 'the good ended happily, and the bad unhappily. That is what Fiction means' (Act II, p. 275). The comedy of manners develops from the larger framework of comedy. Its plot tends to be about young rich people, often aristocratic, whose love lives are the subject of interest; the play depends on verbal wit – often called **repartee**, a term derived from fencing. The conversations are witty battles in which the characters score points off each other. The point of their conversation has less to do with communication than with competition. As the term 'manners' suggests, the language is carefully wrought and decorous, but it disguises self-interest and cynicism. As Cecily Cardew will put it in the play, the manners are a 'shallow mask' (Act II, p. 292). In this play, however, the mask disguises no substance. The characters wear the 'shallow mask of manners' not for purposes of hypocritical disguise; it is simply that there is nothing behind the mask.

The Importance of Being Earnest develops the genre of the **comedy of manners** from its origins in Restoration and eighteenth-century English drama. Other plays in the genre, by William Wycherley (*The Country Wife* – 1674, *The Plain Dealer* – 1676), William Congreve (*The Way of the World* – 1700), John Vanbrugh (*The Relapse* – 1696), or Oliver Goldsmith (*She Stoops to Conquer* – 1773), have plots which revolve around unscrupulous and clever manipulators whose intelligence is rewarded even if their methods and morals are called into question. Oscar Wilde's play uses this kind of framework, but does not encourage moral judgements to be made about the characters. At the end of the play, we might be sure that Algernon Moncrieff is very greedy when it comes to cucumber sandwiches and muffins; but this is not so much a moral failure as a comic foible – the audience is not invited to judge him, just to laugh at him. One of the ways of thinking about the play, then, is as a drama which uses the conventions of the comedy of manners in its conversational strategies; but which uses those conventions with the intention of producing **farce**, a purely comic form where no morality is implied.

This apparent absence or subversion of serious values explains why *Earnest* has been described (by the playwright and cultural historian

Neil Bartlett) as 'the finest flower of English camp'. It is important to recall that the play's subtitle is *A Trivial Comedy for Serious People*. The word **camp** mixes up the trivial and the serious. It is used to describe both a mode of behaviour (a deliberately affected or ostentatious manner, for example) and a serious attitude to works of art or literature whose status is dubious; it is also largely – in the popular mind, at least – associated with homosexuality.

Throughout its length, the play takes the serious and upends it. Questions about the relationships between the sexes, marriage, social position and proper behaviour arise during the course of the conversations which make up the play. But in every case they are treated as jokes, as if they do not matter. This is the fun of the play, and it is also one of the things that can be analysed – despite Archer's anxieties that there's no substance to *Earnest*. By not raising any principle the play asks questions about what plays are for: is morality a central criterion for thinking about an artwork, or is morality an irrelevance? Perhaps form matters more than content; perhaps entertainment is as important as instruction in literature. Oscar Wilde probably thought so; but such views very much go against the grain of traditional nineteenth-century ideas about literature, drama and art. *The Importance of Being Earnest* asks its audiences to think about these issues – but only if we choose to do so. The issues are important, both for the late-Victorian period and for contemporary readers and audiences. To treat the important things as if they are jokes is a political strategy because it opens up the possibility that we might question conventional morality, even if we are smiling while we do so.

We also have the choice not to see the politics if we do not wish to. Richard Ellmann, Oscar Wilde's best biographer, argues that Oscar Wilde was a writer who liked habitually to have his cake and eat it too. *The Importance of Being Earnest* is a significant as well as a pleasurable play because it chooses two apparently incompatible modes for drama – it is both a **social critique** and a **farce**. The criticisms it raises about society, the jokes it tells and its experiment with dramatic form are all reasons why it remains important to read it, to see it, to laugh at and with it – and after we've taken our pleasure, we are invited also to think about its more radical implications.

CHECK THE BOOK
One of the best definitions of 'camp' is to be found in Susan Sontag's essay, 'Notes on Camp', in *The Susan Sontag Reader*. Sontag uses *Earnest* as a keynote text throughout her discussion of the term.

CHECK THE BOOK
Neil Sammels in *Wilde Style: The Plays and Prose of Oscar Wilde* (2000) contrasts the apparent frivolity of *Earnest* with the far more didactic dramas of his contemporary and fellow Irishman, George Bernard Shaw. Both playwrights are political writers, he suggests, but they locate the politics of their plays very differently – Shaw preaches at his audiences whereas Wilde made the drama's style into the locus of his political critique.

PART TWO

THE TEXT

CHECK THE FILM

Oliver Parker's film version of the play, for which he also wrote the screenplay, is partially based on the longer four-act version. Its opening scenes show Algy running from pillar to post in London, in an attempt to escape his creditors, and Parker restores the debt-collecting episode at Jack's country house from the four-act version of the play.

CHECK THE BOOK

An account of Wilde's trials can be found in H. Montgomery Hyde's *Famous Trials 7: Oscar Wilde*, which offers a lucid account of the background to his arrest and imprisonment, a summary of the legal situation for homosexual men in the late nineteenth century, and substantial material from the trials themselves.

NOTE ON THE TEXT

Oscar Wilde originally conceived *The Importance of Being Earnest* as a play in four acts. The material which is now in the Act II was originally split between two acts, and expanded by a sub-plot in which Algy is nearly arrested for Ernest's debts on his arrival at Jack's country house. At this stage Algy is impersonating Ernest, Jack's 'wicked' (Act II, p. 277) brother, who of course does not exist, and the bailiffs seek to arrest him until Jack pays off the debts. These are Jack's own debts, contracted whilst he was in London, also impersonating his own wicked brother, Ernest. Jack agrees to pay the necessary money only after Cecily's intervention on Algy/Ernest's behalf, just at the bailiffs are trying to take him away.

Other more minor differences between the four-act and the three-act version include cuts in exchanges which predict plot elements, and changes that sharpen up the conversational pace and manner. The play was cut at the suggestion of George Alexander, the first director of the play in 1895, and the three-act text is the most usually reprinted and performed version, partly because it is the version that Oscar Wilde himself oversaw for publication in 1899.Shortly after the first performances of *Earnest*, Oscar Wilde was arrested and eventually imprisoned for gross indecency.

The disgrace of his criminal trial and conviction meant a relatively long delay between early performances and the first publication of the play which only appeared in a single-volume edition (of the three-act version) in 1899, published by Leonard Smithers and Co. This edition has been the basis for most subsequent published versions of the play, starting with Robert Ross's editions of *The Complete Works of Oscar Wilde*, in fourteen volumes, first published by Methuen in 1908.

The best easily available edition of the three-act version is the New Mermaids edition of 1980, edited by Russell Jackson, which has an excellent introduction and exhaustive notes on the text. A similarly useful scholarly edition is the version reproduced in *The Writings of Oscar Wilde*, edited by Isobel Murray (Oxford University Press, 1989), which also contains other works by Oscar Wilde and provides a useful introduction in the context of some of Oscar Wilde's other works. Oxford University Press also publishes a paperback edition of Oscar Wilde's plays edited by Peter Raby, with extensive notes, suggestions for performance and an appendix containing the omissions from the four-act play; Routledge publishes a further scholarly edition, edited by Joseph Bristow in the English Text Series. A cheaper version is the Penguin Plays edition, *The Important of Being Earnest and Other Plays* (1986), simply a version of the three-act text, with the texts of his other plays, but with no critical apparatus. Penguin have also published *Earnest* in a single volume.

CHECK THE BOOK
Sos Eltis discusses Wilde's own alterations to the play as he drafted it through various stages from late summer 1894 to its original performance in 1895. See *Revising Wilde: Society and Subversion in the Plays of Oscar Wilde*.

In 1956, the four-act version was rediscovered and published for the first time. It appears that Oscar Wilde had sent his original play-script to an American impresario some time towards the end of 1894, but no American production took place because of his disgrace. The manuscript disappeared for many years, and only came to light in the 1950s. If you are interested in comparing this version to the three-act version, the second edition of *The Complete Works of Oscar Wilde*, edited by Oscar Wilde's grandson, Merlin Holland (Harper Collins, 1994) is the most widely available edition for you to consult. As well as almost all of Oscar Wilde's published work, this volume also has good scholarly introductions to the texts, and a bibliography of Oscar Wilde's works and of works about him.

The edition used in these Notes is the Penguin Plays edition, *The Important of Being Earnest and Other Plays*, 1986.

SYNOPSIS

The play is set in contemporary (1890s) England, and is a story about love and marriage amongst the upper classes. Algernon Moncrieff (known usually as Algy) and John Worthing (known as Jack in the country and Ernest in town) are two rich and idle young men, in romantic pursuit of two similarly wealthy and upper-class

CONTEXT

The setting of the play closely mirrors the class and social standing of the audiences who made up the spectators of the play's original performance.

young women, Cecily Cardew (Jack's ward) and Gwendolen Fairfax (Algy's cousin) respectively. The plot, such as it is, is taken up with a series of delays to the expected resolution in marriage for all the young people. The delays are comic, arising from trivial misunderstandings between the lovers and the snobbish attitudes of Gwendolen's mother, Lady Bracknell.

The play opens in Algy's rooms in Half-Moon Street where he is awaiting the arrival of Lady Bracknell (Gwendolen's mother) and Gwendolen herself, for tea. Before their arrival, Algy's friend, Jack Worthing enters the scene. The two men talk mostly about nothing, though in the course of their conversation they discuss the matter of Jack's lost cigarette case, which Algy has in his possession. On the basis of evidence in the cigarette case's inscription, Jack is forced to admit to the existence of his ward, Cecily, in whom Algy becomes extremely interested.

Before Lady Bracknell's arrival, they also discuss the doubleness of their lives. In order to escape from dull duties in the country, Jack has invented a wicked brother by the name of Ernest who is always getting into scrapes and is therefore in need of constant rescue. In order to escape from his 'duties' in the city (largely made up of dining at Lady Bracknell's house), Algy has become a 'Bunburyist', having invented an invalid friend named Bunbury whose existence and poor health allow him to go to the country whenever he chooses.

When Lady Bracknell arrives, a little later, with Gwendolen, the four of them take tea; and whilst Lady Bracknell and Algy are out of the room, Jack (known to Gwendolen as Ernest) manages to propose. He is accepted almost purely on the grounds that his name is Ernest, it having always been Gwendolen's dream to marry a man with that name. Lady Bracknell is not, however, prepared to permit their engagement, especially when she finds out that Jack was a foundling child, discovered in a handbag left at the cloakroom at Victoria station.

She tells Jack that there will be no marriage until he acquires some respectable relations, and sweeps from the room. Gwendolen sneaks back, and gets Jack's country address from him, unwittingly overheard by Algy, who now knows the whereabouts of little

Cecily. The curtain falls with Algy planning a Bunburying expedition to Hertfordshire to make Cecily's acquaintance.

Act II opens in the garden of Jack's country house in Hertfordshire, where Cecily is engaged very desultorily in her lessons with her governess, Miss Prism, an elderly lady who is comically infatuated with the local parson, Canon Chasuble. Miss Prism is persuaded to take a constitutional walk with the Canon on the grounds of a fictitious headache, and Cecily is left alone with her thoughts and her diary. She is interrupted by the arrival of Algy, who claims the identity of Ernest Worthing, her uncle Jack's non-existent brother. They proceed to engage in flirtatious conversation before leaving the scene to enter the house so that Algy might have something to eat.

Canon Chasuble and Miss Prism re-enter, engaged in a very different kind of flirtatious conversation, when they are interrupted by the arrival of Jack, dressed in deep mourning clothes. He announces the death of his wicked brother, and arranges a christening for himself to take the name of Ernest, just as Cecily re-enters to announce that Ernest is, in fact, in the dining room. Cecily, still innocent of the deception that has been practised on her, forces a meeting and a 'reconciliation' between the two 'brothers', who are then left alone on the stage to make up their differences. When Jack goes to change out of his mourning dress, Cecily re-enters and receives Algy's proposal, which she accepts because, just like Gwendolen, it has always been her dream to marry a man by the name of Ernest. At this, Algy rushes off to Canon Chasuble to arrange a christening for himself under the name of Ernest.

Cecily, alone on the scene, then receives the visit of Miss Gwendolen Fairfax. The two of them appear to be getting on very well until they each realise that they are both engaged to Ernest Worthing, at which they become bitter and deadly rivals, at least in conversational terms. Their confusion and animosity are cleared up by the reappearance of the two men, who are each correctly identified as Jack Worthing and Algernon Moncrieff. The two women withdraw in sisterly dignity to the house, angry with the men for their deceit, leaving the tea-table and the garden to the men, who eat all the muffins whilst they wonder what to do next.

CONTEXT
The foundling child is a staple feature of much Victorian fiction and drama. The fact of having been 'found' immediately throws suspicion on the respectability of Jack's origins, for there was a strong presumption in Victorian fictions that foundling children were likely to be the illegitimate offspring of illicit sexual encounters.

Act III opens a scene of reconciliation in the drawing room of the country house, when Algy and Jack announce to Cecily and Gwendolen that they are about to be christened to satisfy their mistresses' ideals. Just as they all fall into each other's arms, however, Lady Bracknell arrives and puts a stop to the happy scene. She again forbids the engagement between Jack and Gwendolen, but is stopped in her tracks by the news that Cecily is an heiress, immediately seeing her as a suitable match for her nephew, Algy. As Cecily's guardian, however, Jack forbids the engagement unless he is to be allowed to marry Gwendolen. At this Lady Bracknell prepares to leave in high dudgeon with her daughter, until she accidentally hears the name of Miss Prism, spoken by Canon Chasuble, and demands that the lady be sent for. Her reason is that Miss Prism was once the nurse in her sister's family, and some twenty-eight years before, had lost the baby she was in charge of. It becomes clear, in the course of Miss Prism's stumbling story, that the baby in question is now the young man known as Jack Worthing. He was originally christened Ernest Moncrieff, and is Algy's elder brother, Lady Bracknell's nephew and Gwendolen's cousin.

CHECK THE BOOK

As Kerry Powell notes in *Oscar Wilde and the Theatre of the 1890s*, this is the standard ending to a farce – the title is spoken as a punchline to the proceedings.

All objections to his marriage to Gwendolen – particularly Lady Bracknell's disgust that he should have been bred in a handbag, and Gwendolen's insistence that she can only marry a man by the name of Ernest – are now at an end. The curtain comes down on three embracing couples, Cecily and Algy, Jack and Gwendolen, and Canon Chasuble and Miss Prism, with Jack declaiming that he has learned 'the vital Importance of Being Earnest' (Act III, p. 313) to a glaring Lady Bracknell.

DETAILED SUMMARIES

ACT I

- Algy and Jack converse about their double lives and take tea.
- When Lady Bracknell and Gwendolen arrive a little later, Jack manages to propose to Gwendolen and is accepted, but he is thwarted in his desires by Lady Bracknell's intervention and her insistence that he acquire respectable relatives.
- Algy discovers Jack's country address, and arranges to go Bunburying in pursuit of 'little Cecily'.

The play opens in Algy's London rooms in Half Moon Street. The stage directions emphasise the room's luxurious and artistic furnishings, and they place the scene in contemporary (1890s) London, and amongst the wealthy upper classes. When the curtain rises, Lane, the butler, is alone on the stage, arranging things for tea, and Algy, it is to be inferred, is offstage playing the piano in an adjoining room. The tone of the play is set in the opening exchanges between Algy and Lane – it is clear from their light-hearted discussions of marriage and champagne that this is a comic world where nothing need be taken too seriously. The tea-table that is being prepared by Lane is in readiness for the arrival of Lady Bracknell and Gwendolen, her daughter. Before the arrival of the invited guests, however, Ernest Worthing (known in the country as Jack) is shown into the room by Lane; Jack makes himself at home, tries to eat some of the cucumber sandwiches, but is prevented by Algy who insists that they are for the entertainment of his aunt, though he then proceeds to eat them all himself. Jack tells Algy that he has come to London expressly to propose to Gwendolen. Algy tells Jack that such a marriage is impossible, particularly because Jack is clearly leading a secret life.

The evidence for this is Jack's cigarette case, lost some time before, and now in Algy's possession. The inscription in the cigarette case is addressed to Uncle Jack (not to Ernest), and signed from 'little Cecily'.

> **CONTEXT**
>
> The idea of the double or secret life was a recurrent theme in late Victorian writing, though it was generally treated with far more seriousness, and as a matter for moral panic. In Robert Louis Stevenson's *The Strange Case of Dr Jekyll and Mr Hyde* (1886), for example, the double is a terrifying emanation of the respectable Dr Jekyll's dark psychology; and Wilde himself had made more serious use of the figure of doubling in his only novel, *The Picture of Dorian Gray* (1890–1). The terrifying Jack the Ripper murders in the East End of London in 1888–9 were commonly supposed (probably wrongly) to be the work of an upper-class man who was leading a double life.

CONTEXT

Isobel Murray's edition of the play notes the fact that the name Bunbury is a private joke. Wilde actually had a friend named Henry S. Bunbury.

There is much comic stage business with the cigarette case, with Jack trying to get it back and Algy withholding it until he forces his friend to admit who 'little Cecily' is. Jack explains that she is his ward, left in his care by his own guardian, Mr Thomas Cardew. He is known as Ernest in town and as Jack in the country because he finds country life so dull that he needs a good excuse to escape sometimes to London. Ernest is the name of his brother, whom Jack has made up. This fictitious brother is very wicked, is always getting into trouble and is always in need of rescue, thereby providing Jack with the perfect excuse for doing exactly what he likes. Algy names this deceit an act of 'Bunburyism', explaining that Bunbury is the name of a fictitious invalid he has invented in order to be able to escape to the country whenever the duties of city living become too much.

The two men engage in good-natured argument about their behaviour; then the doorbell rings, announcing the invited guests. Before Lady Bracknell and Gwendolen enter, Algy agrees to get Lady Bracknell out of the way so that Jack can propose to her provided that Jack invites him out to dine that night – Algy is a man who likes his food.

CONTEXT

Lady Bracknell's interrogation of Jack is a parody of the standard questions that might be asked of any upper-class young man seeking to marry an upper-class young woman. The questions should, more properly, be addressed by the girl's father rather than her mother.

During the conversation between the two men, the tea-table has been decimated, and there are no cucumber sandwiches left for the new arrivals. Lady Bracknell is unworried by this, though we can infer from the fact she merely bows to Jack with 'icy coldness' (p. 261) and does not speak to him, that she is displeased to find him there. In the course of their conversation, Algy disengages himself from dinner at his aunt's house, using the excuse of Bunbury's failing health, and he gets his aunt out of the room by suggesting that he will help her with the choice of music for her last reception of the year. The coast is now clear for Jack to make his rather halting proposal to Gwendolen. In the course of their discussion, Jack discovers that Gwendolen has a passion for the name of Ernest, and is thrown into a panic about this since his real name is Jack. He eventually proposes all the same, and the couple are just about to indulge in a rapturous embrace when Lady Bracknell returns from the adjoining room. She is not in the least pleased by the news of her daughter's engagement, dismisses Gwendolen from the room, and proceeds to interrogate Jack about his suitability as a husband.

The catechism goes well until Jack has to admit that he has no parents nor any relations, but that he was found in a 'hand-bag' in the cloakroom of Victoria Station. Lady Bracknell's disgust is comically exaggerated, but there can be no doubt that she means it when she says that there can be no marriage between her daughter and 'a parcel' (p. 269), and that Jack must acquire some respectable relatives if he is to stand any chance of union with Gwendolen. She then sweeps majestically from the room.

Algy meanwhile is still offstage, from where he begins to play an enthusiastic version of the Wedding March, to Jack's fury. Jack explains that Gwendolen is perfectly happy about marrying him, but that Lady Bracknell disapproves. Algy wonders whether Jack has told the truth, either about his dual identity, or about his ward – Jack, of course, has done no such thing. Their conversation is interrupted by Gwendolen's re-entry. She has sneaked away from her mother in order to discover Jack's country address from him. Algy carefully eavesdrops and writes the address on his shirt-cuff – this is how he will be able to find little Cecily and see if she is as interesting as he thinks she might be.

Whilst Jack is offstage escorting Gwendolen to her awaiting carriage, he lays plans for a Bunburying trip, asking Lane to pack his things, and the curtain falls as he smugly smokes and smilingly reads Jack's Hertfordshire address off his cuff.

COMMENTARY

Like the rest of the play, this Act is very closely constructed. The opening exchanges between Algy and Lane establish the tone – light-hearted, witty and beyond the reach of conventional morality. Like much of the rest of the play, Algy's relationship with Lane depends on a witty reversal of expected social norms. The 1890s was an era in which, in the proper upper or middle-class home, the assumption was that a high moral tone was transmitted from masters to servants. In this context, however, whilst Lane is clearly in a subordinate social position, serving Algy and obeying his orders, their conversational exchanges imply equality of wit, if not of social standing. Lane behaves as the exemplary servant who sees and hears nothing of his master's peccadilloes: for example, he 'didn't think it polite to listen' (p. 253) to Algy's piano playing.

CONTEXT

In the nineteenth century, men's shirts were commonly made with detachable cuffs and collars, often made of the new material of celluloid – a good surface for writing on, at least if one wrote in pencil.

CONTEXT

In real life, the middle and upper classes must have lived under fairly severe restraints, since their every action – even within the privacy of their homes – was observed by those who served them. In Victorian England, the phrase 'pas devant', a contraction of the French phrase 'pas devant les enfants' [not in front of the children] was extended to include servants who were not be permitted to observe the failings, outbursts of temper, or any kind of impropriety on the part of their so-called 'betters'.

ACT I continued

CONTEXT
The gap between appearance and reality is a major theme in Wilde's work – and, by extension, in his life. As he wrote in a series of epigrams published as 'Phrases and Philosophies for the Use of the Young': 'In all unimportant matters, style, not sincerity, is the essential. In all important matters, style not sincerity, is the essential.' Wilde self-plagiarizes in repeating this remark in *Earnest*, where it is spoken by Gwendolen at the beginning of Act III (see p. 301).

But this is also a joke which at the same time as speaking of his status as a servant, also implies a critique of Algy's musical ability (as Algy says himself, 'I don't play accurately ... but I play with wonderful expression'), narrowing the social gap between them (p. 253).

Moreover, although Lane is unfailingly polite and deferential in his manner, the content of what he says is at least faintly at odds with his obsequious appearance.

He does not become annoyed by Algy's implication that the servants – presumably including Lane himself – have drunk all the champagne; he sees it not as an insult on his professionalism, but as an opportunity to express his views on the difference between bachelor establishments and the homes of married couples. As Algy comments, Lane's views on marriage are very lax compared to the strictly moral views he might have been expected to hold. He is shocked that the lower orders do not provide a better example to his own class, a direct reversal of the usual assumptions about the transmission of morality. Lane also acts on his own initiative. Later in the Act, when Algy discovers that there are no cucumber sandwiches left for Lady Bracknell because he has already eaten them all, Lane comes to his rescue, concocting a story about there having been no cucumbers to buy at the market that day, not even for 'ready money' (as opposed to the credit transactions by which Algy presumably usually maintains his lavish lifestyle – p. 261). He is clearly also a very trusted servant, entirely in on the secret of the fictitious Bunbury.

Whilst Lane is a very minor character, his existence establishes both the tone and the social context of the play. It cannot be a serious play if the servants are in some senses the equals of their masters; and it must be a particularly comfortable social class that can afford such good service. When thinking about his role, you should also compare him to Jack's servant in the country, Merriman, and look in particular for points of comparison between them.

The reader/spectator should also think carefully about the setting of the play. Oscar Wilde's stage direction tells us that Algy's bachelor pad is 'luxuriously and artistically furnished' (p. 253). This is a vague description, but the visual impact of the opening scene is nonetheless important for how the spectator views the tone of the play. Most of Oscar Wilde's contemporaries on the London stage of the 1890s were writing **naturalistic** dramas: that is, what the viewer saw on the stage was a closely observed reproduction of the scenery of real life, and the actions of the play were actions that could take place in the real world. For plays with a domestic setting, this meant intense attention to details of decor, furnishings, ornaments and even carpets as well as the replication of costume detail from contemporary life. The actors were supposed to resist overt theatricality – no wild gestures, exaggerated movements, unnatural speech or direct addresses to the audience. Oscar Wilde's designation of Algy's rooms could be interpreted either naturalistically or symbolically, and the effect of setting on the tone of the rest of the production would certainly be significant for the ways in which audiences interpret the play. When you look at the play, you need to think about whether it is a naturalistic drama, to be played as if it were a representation of real life, or whether it is a representation of a conventionalised and artificial world. The design of Algy's luxuriously and artistically furnished rooms is one of the places in which that message will first be conveyed. The same point can also be made about the costumes that the characters wear. Costume also operates as a signal as to what kind of character we are seeing, even before the character speaks.

Another of the clues about play world – is it natural or artificial? – is to be found in the language in which the characters speak. Their conversation is highly formalised; it is the speech of an elite social group, and the style of language is at least as important as the substance of what is said. Lady Bracknell's speech, for example, is at once very proper and utterly heartless. It would appear that she carefully observes social niceties with no regard for conventional morality, as in her speech about Bunbury's illness. Her concern about Bunbury relies entirely on the fact that his illness might disrupt her own social schedule because it takes Algy away from town.

> Well, I must say, Algernon, that I think it is high time that Mr Bunbury made up his mind whether he was going to live or die. This shilly-shallying with the question is absurd. Nor do I in any way approve of the modern sympathy with invalids. I consider it morbid. Illness of any kind is hardly a thing to be encouraged in

CHECK THE FILM

In both Anthony Asquith's and Oliver Parker's film versions of the play, the costumes of the various characters offer extremely strong visual clues as to the social standing and moral characters of the people who inhabit them. Both Algy and Jack are dandies – men who pay an exaggerated amount of attention to their clothing; and Lady Bracknell and her daughter signal their formidable personalities by being – to modern eyes – remarkably over-dressed. Additionally, in both films, the settings are highly significant, and the viewer is supposed to interpret the details of furniture and décor.

CONTEXT

Invalidism was very differently understood in the Victorian era. In a period where upper- and middle-class women had relatively little autonomy and independence, one way in which they were able to assert control over their own lives was to retreat into the life of the invalid – with illnesses that varied from the purely psychosomatic to those that were life-threateningly real. Victorian fiction abounds with invalid women, of whom the most famous example is possibly Miss Havisham in Dickens' *Great Expectations* (1860–1). But there were also real cases of invalidism – the poet Elizabeth Barrett-Browning and the nurse Florence Nightingale, for example. Lord Bracknell's ill-health therefore represents a comic reversal of the presumption of feminine invalidity and implies his emasculation by his formidable wife.

others. Health is the primary duty of life. I am always telling that to your poor uncle, but he never seems to take much notice … as far as any improvement in his ailment goes. (p. 262, ellipses in original)

As with all the speeches, the reader or spectator needs to think about the tone of this outburst. Notice the way in which Lady Bracknell's speech overturns our assumptions about illness, seeing it as something that the invalid wills on himself, and about which he can make up his mind. She comically sees illness as a moral question that is susceptible to choice as opposed to a physical condition over which the sufferer has no control.

This speech and several others like it establish Lady Bracknell as a comically formidable woman – one certainly has the impression that Lord Bracknell is a henpecked husband who has retreated strategically into illness rather than have to face his wife.

Her speeches are generally very controlled, suggesting that she is a character who likes to be in charge. She brooks no argument. And because she is so powerful, even the most absurd of her assumptions is not open to challenge. She is the site of one the play's major themes, the reversal of power relations between the sexes. Jack is quite right to be worried about whether Gwendolen will turn out to be a gorgon like her mother 'in about a hundred and fifty years' (p. 269) – the similarities between them, signalled in their similar speech patterns and in most productions, in their similar taste in dress, are already very marked. You should also look at the number of places in this Act, and in the play as a whole, in which direct commands produce no action, or when speech contradicts action. The gap between language and reality is an important theme of the play, as for example, when Algy tells Jack not to eat the cucumber sandwiches and promptly eats them himself; or when Algy and Lane lie about the non-existence of cucumbers that morning at the market; or when Algy disobeys Gwendolen's order not to listen to her conversation with Jack towards the end of the Act, and so gains Jack's country address.

These examples all have a comic effect which relies on the audience's assumption that language and reality are related, an assumption which is very often belied by the actions of the play. They also signal important differences between characters such as Algy and Jack. When Jack is given an order, he generally obeys it: he does not eat the cucumber sandwiches, but has the bread and butter instead; he does indeed rise from his 'semi-recumbent posture' (p. 265) in Gwendolen's embrace when ordered to do so by Lady Bracknell. Other characters – in particular Gwendolen and Algy – do not obey orders. Gwendolen, for example, does not follow her mother offstage as she is told to, even though she says she will, when Lady Bracknell and Algy leave the room to discuss music for Lady Bracknell's reception (p. 263). And it is only very reluctantly that she eventually leaves the room and awaits her mother in the carriage during Lady Bracknell's interrogation of Jack (pp. 265–6). It may well be that the clever, powerful characters in the play are those who use language for their own ends, and only hear what they want to hear. Jack and Algy are, on the surface, very similar young men. Comparatively, however, Jack is an innocent abroad, who never wins verbal battles and who always ends up doing what he is told.

Alongside reversals in the social relations between masters and servants, and the conventional relations between the sexes, the play also raises questions about the meanings of masculinity and femininity, that is, what was thought to constitute a real man and a real woman. We've already seen that in this first Act, it is the female characters who appear more powerful than the male characters, in a direct reversal of the conventional power relations between them. The women, that is, especially Lady Bracknell, have masculine power; the men appear comparatively effeminate. This is part of the play's social satire, articulated in the discussion between Jack and Lady Bracknell about his eligibility as a suitor for Gwendolen's hand. The play is set, after all, in the Age of Empire, in which the ideal of the real man was powerfully invested with meaning. A real man of the upper class was supposedly one who had a responsible and well-paid occupation, preferably with the addition of a private income. He worked and played hard; as a 'man of the world' he had wide experience and knowledge, a strong sense of social responsibility and a deep-seated morality.

CONTEXT

In another series of epigrams, 'A Few Maxims for the Instruction of the Over-Educated', Wilde wrote: 'One should never listen. To listen is a sign of indifference to one's hearers.' One of the themes of the play, and of Wilde's work more generally, is the failure of communication.

CONTEXT

All Wilde's social comedies of the 1890s make reference to the concept of ideal masculinity. See especially the speeches by Lady Chiltern on her husband's character in *An Ideal Husband* (1895) in the Penguin Plays volume for an idea of what constituted appropriate manliness in the period.

Of the qualifications for true upper-class manhood, Jack has only money. But Lady Bracknell seems remarkably unmoved that her prospective son-in-law regards smoking as a proper occupation, that he is utterly ignorant, that he is idle and effete. Her objection to him is not his want of character, but his want of respectable relations. Her assumptions, that is, reverse the assumptions of the original audience about what constitutes manliness. Her world is an entirely social world, in which qualities that are not measurable at a dinner-party or reception do not count as qualities at all. And everything that can be said about Jack's character in these respects may also be said of Algy. In this play, the young women are beautiful – but the young men are not manly.

GLOSSARY

Tunbridge Wells (p. 258) once a fashionable resort in Kent, but also a byword for stuffy respectability

the Albany (p. 259) bachelor chambers near Piccadilly

Willis's (p. 259) a fashionable restaurant that would have been known to Oscar Wilde's original audience

Wagnerian manner (p. 260) Lady Bracknell rings the bell loudly. Richard Wagner was a composer famous for impassioned (and therefore very loud) opera

Liberal Unionist (p. 267) as Russell Jackson notes, this is the late-nineteenth-century equivalent of a 'don't know'. The Liberals were the party who had campaigned for Irish Home Rule, and therefore against the Union with Ireland. To be a Liberal Unionist is therefore more or less a contradiction in terms

hand-bag (p. 268) not the item carried today usually by women, but any piece of hand luggage. The bag in question must be quite large in order to fit a baby in it

right as a trivet (p. 269) absolutely fine. A trivet is a metal stand for putting hot dishes on so that the wooden surfaces of furniture are protected. It is proverbially stable because it has three legs

Gorgon (p. 269) proverbially anything unbearably hideous. The gorgons were mythological monsters with snakes for hair whose appearance would turn anyone who saw them to stone

Club (p. 271) gentleman's club, where men met for food, drink and conversation

Empire (p. 271) a popular music-hall, also well-known to Oscar Wilde's original audience

ACT II

- Algy comes to country and proposes to Cecily in the guise of Ernest Worthing.
- Gwendolen comes to the country in pursuit of Jack.
- Miss Prism goes for a walk in amorous pursuit of Canon Chasuble.
- The true identities of the Jack and Algy are unmasked, and the Act closes with an impasse – the men in the garden, the women in the house, each pairing wondering what will happen next.

> **? QUESTION**
> Discuss the ways in which the language of *The Importance of Being Earnest* signals the strengths and weaknesses of the various characters who speak it.

The scene is the garden of Jack Worthing's country estate in Hertfordshire. Miss Prism and Cecily Cardew are supposed to be busy with Cecily's lessons, but Cecily is a reluctant pupil, snatching at any opportunity to delay learning her German grammar. The two women discuss Uncle Jack and his wicked brother Ernest, in whom Cecily is clearly very interested; and Cecily further delays settling to her lessons by writing in her diary for which Miss Prism admonishes her. In the course of their conversation, we learn that Miss Prism had once written a novel, but that the manuscript had been lost.Cecily seizes the opportunity to get rid of her governess for a while when she spies Canon Chasuble in the distance, and she persuades the two of them to go for a stroll. She is left briefly alone, railing against school-work, when Mr Ernest Worthing is announced – it is Algy Moncrieff in disguise. The two of them flirt and then they enter the house, just as Miss Prism and Canon Chasuble return, engaged in earnest conversation about marriage. They are just starting to wonder where Cecily might be when Jack, dressed in deep mourning, enters the scene to explain that he is mourning the death of his brother Ernest, carried off by a severe chill in Paris. Jack also arranges for a christening for himself, that he might take the name of Ernest, and thus retain Gwendolen's affections.

At this moment, Cecily returns to announce that Jack's wicked brother, far from being dead is actually in the dining room. She goes to fetch him, and insists that the two men be reconciled by a handshake. Jack and Algy are then left alone on the stage, all the better to effect their reconciliation. Jack, unsurprisingly, is not reconciled, and insists that Algy return to town by the next train. He goes to change out of his mourning clothes, and Cecily returns. There is more flirtatious conversation between Cecily and Algy, which Cecily copies verbatim into her diary. They are interrupted several times by Merriman, the butler, announcing the arrival of the dog-cart to take Algy to the station, but they parry the injunction that Algy must leave, and he proposes marriage. Cecily announces that they have in fact been engaged for several months – the evidence is in her diary. It has always been her wish to love a man named Ernest, and frustrated by her inability to meet the 'real' Ernest Worthing, she arranged their engagement, with its attendant love letters and tokens by writing about it. Just like Jack, Algy realises that he must change his name, and rushes off to arrange a christening with Canon Chasuble, leaving Cecily alone once more.

CHECK THE FILM

In the Anthony Asquith film, this scene is played to great comic effect, with much unscripted 'business' from the servants, who relish the poor behaviour of their masters.

The arrival of Miss Gwendolen Fairfax is announced, and she is received and given tea by Cecily. The two women appear to get on very well, despite Gwendolen's discomfiture at the discovery that Cecily is not only very young and pretty, but is also a permanent resident at Jack's country house. The calm is shattered however, by the discovery that both women believe that they are engaged to Ernest Worthing. They are unable to vent their spleen at each other because of the presence of servants serving tea, but they engage in very polite hostilities, until Jack and Algy reappear, and are each identified by the women as not being Ernest Worthing at all.

Cecily and Gwendolen sweep into the house in dignified fury, leaving the men in possession of the tea-table with the muffins for consolation: Algy eats the muffins and Jack gets none. The curtain falls with them finishing off the food and wondering what to do next.

COMMENTARY

As with Act I, the setting of Act II is also important. The entire action is set in the garden of Jack's country manor in Hertfordshire, described by Oscar Wilde as '*old-fashioned*' (p. 274) and full of roses. It is a hot July day which is why Cecily and Miss Prism come to be doing their work outside. If one of the themes of the play is the relationship between nature and artifice, a garden is a highly appropriate setting, since it is a place in which nature and culture are situated side by side. It helps to set up the contrast between country and city which is so important to the text, but it also shows that country and city are not direct **binary oppositions** – that is, they are not absolutely contrasted to each other. Although Cecily is described by Algy as being 'like a pink rose' (p. 279), she is not a figure of nature incarnate. The roses in the garden are, after all, cultivated rather than purely natural.

As the scene progresses, the reader and the spectator are brought to the realisation that the conventional associations of the country and the city (nature and innocence versus culture and corruption) do not quite hold true. Whilst Cecily is not so sophisticated as Gwendolen, she is well on her way to becoming very like her. In his critical dialogue 'The Decay of Lying' (published in *Intentions*, 1891), Oscar Wilde argues that nature is, in fact, a human invention, a cultural construction rather than a naturally existing phenomenon. The setting in the garden signals this concern with nature and culture as related facts. They are not seen as simple oppositions which help us easily to identify good and bad, innocence and corruption, morality and depravity.This **ambiguity** is figured in the character of Cecily Cardew, earlier described by Jack as a byword for innocent common-sense attitudes: 'Cecily is not a silly romantic girl, I am glad to say,' Jack tells us: 'She has got a capital appetite, goes long walks, and pays no attention at all to her lessons' (pp. 270–1).

As the events of this Act demonstrate, Jack is sadly mistaken (as he usually is). Cecily is a silly romantic girl who has fallen in love with a name, and invented a courtship and engagement, which she writes into her diary. She is also, at the same time, in the process of learning sophisticated city ways which she puts into practice in her verbal sparring match with Gwendolen. Cecily learns nothing from Miss Prism, but she is learning about the ways of the world – and the apparently innocent country girl certainly holds her own with the female urban sophisticate.

Act II is full of entrances and exits which precipitate some meetings and delay others, in the manner of a **bedroom farce** where meetings and non-meetings are the essence of the comic plot. This is most marked in the passage where Cecily and Algy leave the garden for the house, and are followed immediately into the scene by Canon

> **CONTEXT**
>
> If Lord Bracknell is a comic invalid, whose incapacity reverses one gender stereotype, then Cecily upends another common contemporary presumption – that young ladies are fragile and delicate, and must be cared for with supreme gentleness. In this, as elsewhere in the play, Wilde makes reference to the then scandalous idea of the New Woman. (See Historical background.)

Chasuble and Miss Prism, to whom Jack shortly announces the news of his 'brother's' 'death'. When Cecily re-enters, she refuses to read the serious significance of her uncle's mourning clothes, and announces that Ernest is, in fact, in the dining room. The comedy of this exchange depends on the swiftness of entrance and exits, on the audience's sense of **dramatic irony**. The audience knows more than the characters on-stage and is therefore more aware of the mismatch between appearance and reality. When Jack announces Ernest's death, for example, we learn something of the characters of Miss Prism (her unforgiving response to male vice in her repeated refrain of 'As a man sows, so shall he reap' – p. 280) and Canon Chasuble's more forgiving Christian attitudes. In other contexts these responses would be serious and appropriate; but here they are comic because they have no relationship with the facts as the audience knows them. The two older characters, who ought to be the founts of wisdom and knowledge, representing respectively education and the Church, are rendered foolish and obtuse by the 'true' situation of which they know nothing. The comedy is compounded by Algy and Jack's 'reconciliation', termed a 'beautiful action' (p. 283) by Chasuble because it appears to represent Christian forgiveness. Again there is a gap between what the audience on the stage (Cecily, Miss Prism and Chasuble) know in comparison to the knowledge of the audience in the auditorium or the play's readership.

? QUESTION
Discuss the comic uses of entrances and exits in *The Importance of Being Earnest.*

This farcical structure of revelation and concealment is repeated towards the end of the Act, following the meeting of Cecily and Gwendolen and their hostile conversation after their mutual discoveries that they are each engaged to Ernest Worthing. Again the audience knows that Ernest does not exist; and we respond with gleeful anticipation when Jack and Algy appear on the scene to have their identities revealed to the chagrin of all concerned. The comedy is compounded by the exaggerated, almost melodramatic responses of the two women to the deception. They speak the affected – that is, non-naturalistic – language of **melodrama**: 'My poor wounded Cecily!'; 'My sweet wronged Gwendolen' (p. 295); and they reproduce the actions of melodrama in an exaggerated embrace.

It is important to remember Oscar Wilde's subtitle for the play: *A Trivial Comedy for Serious People.* Several times in Act II, the play takes ideas that the original audience would have regarded very seriously, and mocks them. The most acute example of this is the discussion of Jack's baptism. Baptism is supposed to be a sacrament, one of the most sacred acts of the church according to believers. Jack, however, orders his baptism in much the same way as he would order any other commodity: 'I suppose you know how to christen all right?' he asks. And again, 'I would like to be christened myself, this afternoon, if you have nothing better to do.' He offers to 'trot round at about five' for the ceremony (p. 281). The colloquial, chatty register in which Jack speaks of the sacrament implies that the sacrament is not held in properly high regard. His manner in talking of his own christening contrasts with Miss Prism's and Canon Chasuble's earlier discussion of the importance of marriage – a discussion they hold in all earnestness with reference to the authority of the Primitive Church, but which is nonetheless funny both because of Chasuble's cynicism about affection between husbands and wives (he has heard that married men are often not even attractive to the women they have married – p. 279) and because of Miss Prism's clear self-interest in the conversation: she wants Chasuble to agree that marriage is a good thing because she wants to marry him herself.

The end of the Act, when Algy and Jack are left alone on the stage with the tea-table reprises the scenario of Act I. Again it is Algy who is successful in getting to eat the food he likes; again it is Jack who is really anxious about the results of the afternoon's events, whilst Algy appears unmoved, declaring it 'The most wonderful Bunbury I have ever had in my life' (p. 296). Their conversation demonstrates once again their similarities and differences. They each speak of the loss of the other's excuse for pleasure (Algy's Bunbury is 'quite exploded' (p. 296), Jack's brother is looking 'a little off colour' (p. 297)). They each declare that the other has no chance of marrying the girl of his dreams. But whilst their language and apparent sentiments are similar, Jack is more upset than Algy signalled by the fact that as the curtain drops, Algy is still eating whilst Jack is prostrate and groaning in a garden chair.

QUESTION
In one of his epigrams, Wilde wrote: 'Nothing that actually occurs is of the smallest importance' ('Phrases and Philosophies for the Use of the Young'). Discuss the relevance of this view for a reading of *The Importance of Being Earnest*.

GLOSSARY

Miss Prism (p. 274) Miss Prism's name is a near-pun on the word misprision, meaning misunderstanding.

CHECK THE BOOK

Raymond Williams's *The Country and The City* (1973) is an extended discussion of the ways in which ideas about the countryside and the urban landscape function in culture. It provides a useful overview of this idea that is illuminating on the unconventional use Wilde makes of the opposing spaces.

GLOSSARY CONTINUED

three-volume novels (p. 275) it was usual in the late nineteenth century for novels to be published in three volumes rather than in a single volume edition. The practice was starting to die out by the mid-nineties, suggesting that the novels Miss Prism approves for Cecily to read are rather old-fashioned

Mudie (p. 275) Mudie was the name of one of the circulating libraries in whose interest the three-volume novel had lasted so long (since readers had to pay three times rather than once to borrow any given text). The circulating libraries were notorious for the conservatism of their texts which had to be suitable for ladies and children

Dr Chasuble (p. 276) a chasuble is a priest's vestment, making Dr Chasuble's name utterly suitable for his role

Egeria... Laetitia (p. 276) Egeria was a nymph in Roman mythology who wisely advised a Roman king before becoming his mistress. That Miss Prism doesn't know who she was suggests that she is not a particularly suitable person to be a teacher. Her own name, Laetitia, means 'joy', a name which might be regarded as rather unsuitable for her character

Maréchal Niel (p. 279) a yellow rose

misanthrope... womanthrope (p. 279) a misanthrope is one who dislikes mankind; Miss Prism's coinage 'womanthrope' presumably therefore means woman-hater, for which the more proper term would be 'misogynist'

mourning **(p. 280)** when close relatives died, it was traditional to wear 'mourning' clothes, in black, to signal one's grief. There were strictly graded kinds of mourning, depending on how close the relative who had died, and how long ago the death had taken place

canonical practice (p. 281) canonical practice is any practice which the church holds to be in keeping with its own laws (or canons)

ACT III

- When Jack and Algy announce that they will be christened to satisfy the romantic ideals of their womenfolk, all looks set for a happy ending.

- This is interrupted by Lady Bracknell who continues to forbid Gwendolen's engagement to Jack.

- The resolution comes through the accidental meeting of Miss Prism and Lady Bracknell, and the subsequent discovery of Jack's real identity as Ernest Moncrieff.
- The curtain comes down on three engagements, as Cecily and Algy, Jack and Gwendolen, and Miss Prism and Canon Chasuble all fall into each other's arms.

The opening of Act III takes off from the ending of Act II, with Cecily and Gwendolen in the house, to which they have retired in disgust because neither of the two young men to whom they are engaged is called Ernest; they are looking out of the window at Algy and Jack who remain offstage, in the garden. We know that they are still eating the muffins from the tea-table because the women comment on the fact in their opening remarks. The men do not stay in the garden for long, however, and come in, whistling a tune from a British opera, to face a dignified silence by the women, a silence that lasts a very short time.

Algy and Jack briefly explain that they had pretended to be Ernest Worthing only in order to get close to the women of their dreams, and Cecily and Gwendolen are almost persuaded to forgive them, but for one fact: their Christian names are an 'insuperable barrier' (p. 301) to married bliss. Algy and Jack then explain that they are about to be christened with the name of Ernest, and all looks set for a happy ending. The two couples are all embracing when they are interrupted by the arrival of Lady Bracknell.

Lady Bracknell is very angry, and immediately separates Gwendolen and Jack. She is, however, somewhat mollified by noticing Cecily in Algy's arms, especially when she discovers the extent of Cecily's prospects and property. She gives her blessing to this match, and instructs Cecily to call her Aunt Augusta.

It is, however, now Jack's turn to intervene. He forbids the marriage as Cecily's guardian, explaining that she cannot marry without his permission until she is thirty-five, and that his permission is withheld because Algy's honesty is questionable.

He makes it clear that he will only relent if Lady Bracknell should agree to his engagement to Gwendolen. She indignantly refuses this

CONTEXT

As Richard Ellmann notes in *Oscar Wilde* (1987), the remark that it Jack and Algy whistle 'an air' from a 'dreadful British opera' is a barb aimed at the operettas of Gilbert and Sullivan who had satirized Wilde in their 1882 operetta *Patience*. (See Background.)

CONTEXT

In refusing permission for Cecily to marry, Jack adopts the stock role of the villainous father of the melodrama – a part he is utterly unsuited to play, of course.

proposition, and is preparing to leave when Dr Chasuble enters the room to announce that everything is ready for Jack and Algy's christenings. Lady Bracknell is scandalised by the very suggestion that this should occur, and forbids that the christenings should take place. As Dr Chasuble is sadly leaving he mentions that he will go to the church where Miss Prism is awaiting him. The mention of this name stops Lady Bracknell in her tracks. She demands that Miss Prism be sent for immediately, but the order is forestalled by the arrival of the governess on the scene.Lady Bracknell takes one look at her, and requires of her an explanation for the whereabouts of a baby that she had taken from a house in Upper Grosvenor Square some twenty-eight years before. The perambulator in which the child had been removed had been found, but it contained nothing but the manuscript of a three-volume novel. Miss Prism hesitatingly explains that she does not know where the baby is: in a fit of absent-mindedness, she had placed the manuscript in the baby carriage, and the baby in her hand-bag which she had then deposited in the cloak room of Victoria Station – the Brighton line. When Jack hears this, he rushes upstairs. A great deal of offstage noise is heard before he returns, carrying a hand-bag, which he presents to Miss Prism. She confirms that this was indeed the hand-bag that she had lost. Jack then identifies himself as the baby who had been lost. It takes a while for his true identity to be revealed. At first he assumes that Miss Prism is his mother, but this is not the case. It turns out that he is the elder son of Lady Bracknell's sister and brother-in-law, a high-ranking army officer, and he is consequently Algy's brother and Gwendolen's first cousin. His all-important first name remains a mystery, since Lady Bracknell cannot remember what it was. She knows he was named after his father, but cannot recall the General's name either. Jack swiftly checks the army records for the period, and establishes that his name, after all, is Ernest.

With this discovery, he falls into Gwendolen's arms, since Lady Bracknell's dynastic objections to their marriage have now been overturned, as have Gwendolen's objections to the notoriously homely name of Jack. As Jack and Gwendolen embrace, so do Algy and Cecily, and perhaps more surprisingly, Canon Chasuble and Miss Prism also clasp each other in ecstasy. The curtain drops on this happy tableau, with only Lady Bracknell outside the circle of the hugging couples.

CHECK THE FILM

Oliver Parker's version of *Earnest* ends with Judi Dench as Lady Bracknell noting that the entry in the army lists in fact informs us that Jack's father's name was really John, not Ernest. By this point, however, she has been won over, and connives in the concealment of this important fact from her daughter.

COMMENTARY

Act III is the shortest of the play's divisions, in which the various complications of the plot are relatively speedily resolved. The quick pace of the Act is important, once again aligning the play to the genre of farce. For although the play is about such serious issues as marriage and love, these themes are treated comically, and their seriousness is undermined in part by the cavalier ways in which they are dispatched.

When Jack and Algy enter the house, Gwendolen and Cecily both require explanations of them as to why they have each claimed to be the non-existent Ernest Worthing. Their replies are virtually identical – they have practised deceit in order to gain access to the two women. To both women, this response is satisfactory, presumably because it flatters their vanity: but both claim not quite to believe their suitors, whilst being prepared nonetheless to forgive them. As Gwendolen says, 'In matters of grave importance, style, not sincerity, is the vital thing' (p. 301). Her statement reverses the usual view that sincerity matters more than style; in this world, it is the beauty of the statements, not their reality, that is persuasive. In this view, there is a family resemblance between Gwendolen and her cousin Algy who had commented in Act I about one of his own remarks, 'It is perfectly phrased! and quite as true as any observation in civilized life should be' (p. 270) – the cousins both believe in style over substance.

But the two women are forgetting the 'principle' at stake in their relationships with Algy and Jack – the vital importance of the name of Ernest, which is comically elevated to a principle rather than a preference, debunking the very idea of principles, which are certainly not supposed to be negotiable, and which are supposed to be universal rather than personal. These **paradoxical** reversals of standards are a common verbal strategy throughout the play. Norms of morality or behaviour are often evoked merely to be laughed at (as we saw in Act I with Lady Bracknell's questioning of Jack's propriety as a prospective son-in-law). Language, once again, is divorced from social realities and from accepted moral standards, implying that nothing that happens in the play-world actually matters at all.

These ideas are repeated throughout the Act. For example, when Cecily is told that she will have to wait until she is thirty-five to marry Algy, and he promises romantically to wait for her, she responds:

I couldn't wait all that time. I hate waiting even five minutes for anybody. It always makes me rather cross. I am not punctual myself, I know, but I do like punctuality in others, and waiting, even to be married, is quite out of the question. (p. 307)

Her response contrasts with Algy's romantic declaration that he could wait for her; but it also dramatises the internal contradictions between overt statements of belief and actual actions with which the play is concerned. There is a gap between Cecily's stated desire for punctuality and her failure to be punctual herself – a gap which aligns her neatly with Algy, a man who will tell others not to eat the cucumber sandwiches before promptly eating them himself. Reality, language and belief do not cohere, a point comically reiterated by Lady Bracknell's declaration that they must go: 'we have already missed five, if not six, trains. To miss any more might expose us to comment on the platform' (p. 308). There is no reality here. One only misses a train that one has deliberately intended to catch – and Lady Bracknell has not intended to catch any of the five or six that have departed since her arrival in Hertfordshire; moreover, who can possibly comment on the platform about the impropriety of missing so many trains? Who will know how many have been missed? And in what sense is missing a train a social scandal giving rise to public 'comment'?

QUESTION Consider the view that Lady Bracknell uses language as social weapon.

There is a glorious illogicality about Lady Bracknell, an inconsequential response to language and its effects. Whilst Jack is recovering Miss Prism's hand-bag with a great deal of noise upstairs and offstage, she observes that the noise he is making is 'extremely unpleasant. It sounds as if he was having an argument. I dislike arguments of any kind. They are always vulgar, and often convincing' (p. 310). If an argument is convincing, it ought, logically, to produce an action consistent with the outcome of the argument. Lady Bracknell implies that this will never be the case for her. Arguments are vulgar and so can be legitimately be ignored even when they are right – once again, the relationships between language and reality have been effectively disrupted. The tone of **farce** is reinforced because both the men and the women speak in unison in the opening encounter of the Act. Gwendolen even beats time as she and Cecily inform the men, speaking together, 'Your Christian names are still an insuperable barrier' to marriage

(p. 301); and Jack and Algy reply in unison that they are to be christened that afternoon.

This exchange emphasises the sense that the language of the play is artificial and bears only the slightest relation to any reality that the audience might recognise. Moreover, their discussion is filled with stylised gestures (carried over from Act II, where Cecily and Gwendolen fell **melodramatically** into each other's arms when they discovered treachery of their suitors) implying an artistic choreography of movement rather than natural movements. Not only does Gwendolen 'conduct' her speech with Cecily, but Jack and Algy melodramatically shake hands as they explain their determination to brave the 'dangers' of baptism for the sake of their loves, and then they fall into the arms of their respective fiancées in a kind of quadrille (a four-way dance).

The symmetry of the relationships between the two women and the two men, as well as between the couples they make up across the sex divide is broken up here, as it will be at the end of the play by the figure of Lady Bracknell, who never embraces anyone. Her entry to break up the happy party is signalled by the cough of the butler, Merriman. As he announces her entry, the couples break apart in alarm, the stage direction tells us, suggesting a stage picture of chaos which disrupts the artificial order that the courting couples had established. This predicts the final tableau of the play in which there will be three embracing couples – Gwendolen and Jack, Algy and Cecily and Miss Prism and Canon Chasuble – but where Lady Bracknell will disrupt the symmetry of the image by having no part in it. The positions of figures on the stage operate as a sign of their meanings. Lady Bracknell's interrupting role (reprised here from Act I, when she also separated Gwendolen and Jack) may indeed be her entire function in the play. She is a figure who delays the happy resolution of marriage merely by her very inhibiting presence.

> **? QUESTION**
> To what extent does the staging of *The Importance of Being Earnest* demand intricate choreography?

Moreover, when one looks at the length of Lady Bracknell's speeches in comparison to those of other characters, it is clear that when she is on the stage, she dominates the dialogue. Her language is very measured and deliberate, and her speeches must therefore be delivered slowly. Compared to the pace of the rest of the action of this Act, it starts to become clear that Lady Bracknell is out to

QUESTION

Jack Worthing regards Lady Bracknell as an enemy and as a monster (he calls her a 'gorgon'). But audiences often regard her as the play's heroine. Which view of her do you hold? Give reasons for your answer by close textual reference to the play's text and/or a performance you have seen.

prolong the play be preventing resolution, both physically (by her very presence) and verbally (keeping the scene going by continuing to speak). She also functions to delay resolution by ignoring what appears to be the issue at stake in her concentrated attention to Cecily and Algy. Her attention to the younger woman, her delight in Cecily's profile and appearance as well as her 'most attractive' fortune (p. 304) all put off her projected departure from the scene, and it also delays the resolution of the main issue: whether her daughter and Jack might have any future.

If Lady Bracknell is a static presence, Jack, in particular, becomes very active. The scene is interrupted by the arrival of Canon Chasuble, anxious about the delay to the projected christenings, which are immediately forbidden by the formidable lady. When he seeks to leave to meet Miss Prism, Lady Bracknell does not move, but commands him to remain, and demands Miss Prism's presence: her stillness is her power. When Miss Prism arrives to explain the loss of the baby, it is Jack who is galvanised into action. He rushes upstairs to fetch the hand-bag in which he had originally been found; he makes a great deal of noise in fetching it, and moves swiftly to and from the scene. And to discover his Christian name, he also 'Rushes to [the] bookcase and tears the books out' (p. 312), becoming in the process an **ironic** version of the 'man of action' of proper masculinity. Lady Bracknell's power decreases in direct relation to Jack's energy. As far as possible, Lady Bracknell will not help him to find out who he is. She has to be prompted to explain that he is her nephew, and Algy's brother, and she (perhaps wilfully) cannot remember her brother-in-law's first name. From start to finish, she inhibits the action of the play (its love plot), and insistently defers its resolution.

Apart from Jack and Lady Bracknell, the other characters have relatively little to do in this scene. For much of the time, they are cast rather as observers of a plot which does not seem to involve them. In other words, one might say, there is an audience on the stage as well as an audience off the stage. The offstage audience (and the play's readers) have to observe these observers as well as the main players, and observe their responses to what is played out before them. You should think carefully about how the internal audience reacts to the main action.

GLOSSARY

German scepticism (p. 301) scepticism means a tendency to disbelieve, especially to have doubts about prevailing morals and religious beliefs. The dislike of German is a running joke through the play, with Cecily hating her German grammar because it makes her look ugly, and Lady Bracknell preferring German music at her receptions because it sounds so 'respectable'

University Extension Scheme (p. 302) lectures performed by university staff for the general public as opposed to being part of the formal university curriculum. The University of London was one of the first institutions in the country to provide such a scheme of extramural teaching. The lectures were largely attended by working men whose class status made it difficult to go to university, and by middle-class women who were debarred from formal entry into higher education

revolutionary outrage (p. 303) the contemporary term for what would now be called an act of terrorism. There had been Fenian (Irish Nationalist) and Anarchist outrages during the 1880s and 1890s; and Oscar Wilde himself had had the performance of one of his first plays (*Vera, or The Nihilists*) cancelled following the anarchist assassination of the Russian Czar in 1882

the Sporran, Fifeshire, N.B. (p. 304) Cecily's third address is in Scotland – N.B. stands for North Britain, an old-fashioned and frankly insulting way of designating Scotland. Similarly, Fife is the proper designation of the county, not Fifeshire. The joke is compounded by the house name of Sporran; a sporran is an ornamental pouch of leather and fur, worn from the front of the kilt in traditional Highland dress

Court Guides (p. 304) an annual publication which served a similar purpose to *Who's Who* or *Debrett's*. It listed the names and addresses of the British aristocracy, and it could be assumed that those whose names appeared in it had been presented at court, a mark of respectability

in the Funds (p. 304) Government stocks, which yielded a reliable income with little risk

Oxonian (p. 306) one who has been a student at Oxford University

Anabaptists (p. 308) a Christian sect which rejects infant baptism, and holds that those who have been baptised as children must be baptised again. In context, Dr Chasuble's remark implies that he does not really know what an Anabaptist is

bassinette (p. 312) perambulator (pram) or baby carriage

Army Lists (p. 312) an official list of the names of all commissioned army officers, published annually

? QUESTION In response to Jack's fear that Gwendolen might turn out like her mother, Algy comments: 'All women become like their mothers. That is their tragedy' (p. 270). To what extent is it fair to suggest that Gwendolen is her mother's daughter?

EXTENDED COMMENTARIES

TEXT 1 – ACT I (PP. 256–8)

ALGY DISCOVERS THAT JACK IS LEADING A DOUBLE LIFE

[*Enter* LANE *with the cigarette case on a salver.* ALGERNON *takes it at once.* LANE *goes out.*]

ALGERNON: I think that is rather mean of you, Ernest, I must say. [*Opens case and examines it.*] However, it makes no matter, for, now that I look at the inscription inside, I find that the thing isn't yours after all.

JACK: Of course it's mine! [*Moving to him.*] You have seen me with it a hundred times, and you have no right whatsoever to read what is written inside. It is a very ungentlemanly thing to read a private cigarette case.

ALGERNON: Oh! it is absurd to have a hard and fast rule about what one should read and what one shouldn't. More than half of modern culture depends on what one shouldn't read.

JACK: I am quite aware of the fact, and I don't propose to discuss modern culture. It isn't the sort of thing one should talk of in private. I simply want my cigarette case back.

ALGERNON: Yes; but this isn't your cigarette case. This cigarette case is a present from someone of the name of Cecily, and you said you didn't know anyone of that name.

JACK: Well, if you want to know, Cecily happens to be my aunt.

ALGERNON: Your aunt!

JACK: Yes. Charming old lady she is, too. Lives at Tunbridge Wells. Just give it back to me Algy.

ALGERNON [*retreating to back of sofa*]: But why does she call herself little Cecily if she is your aunt and lives at Tunbridge Wells? [*Reading.*] 'From little Cecily with her fondest love.'

JACK [*moving to sofa and kneeling upon it*]: My dear fellow, what on earth is there in that? Some aunts are tall, some aunts are not tall. That is a matter that surely an aunt may be allowed to decide for herself. You seem to think that every aunt should be exactly like your aunt! That is absurd. For Heaven's sake give me back my cigarette case. [*Follows* ALGERNON *round the room.*]

ALGERNON: Yes. But why does your aunt call you her uncle? 'From little Cecily, with her fondest love to her dear Uncle Jack.' There is no objection, I admit, to an aunt being a small aunt, but why an aunt, no matter what her size may be, should call her own nephew her uncle, I can't quite make out. Besides, your name isn't Jack at all; it is Ernest.

JACK: It isn't Ernest; it's Jack.

ALGERNON: You have always told me it was Ernest. I have introduced to you to every one as Ernest. You answer to the name of Ernest. You look as if your name was Ernest. You are the most earnest-looking person I ever saw in my life. It is perfectly absurd your saying that your name isn't Ernest. It's on your cards. Here is one of them. [*Taking it from case.*] 'Mr Ernest Worthing, B.4, The Albany'. I'll keep this as a proof that your name is Ernest if you ever attempt to deny it to me, or to Gwendolen, or to anyone else. [*Puts the card in his pocket.*]

> **CONTEXT**
> Tunbridge Wells, a prosperous town in Kent, has long been a byword for respectability and conservative values.

JACK: Well, my name is Ernest in town and Jack in the country, and the cigarette case was given to me in the country.

ALGERNON: Yes, but that does not account for the fact that your small Aunt Cecily who lives at Tunbridge Wells, calls you her dear uncle. Come, old boy, you had much better have the thing out at once.

JACK: My dear Algy, you talk exactly as if you were a dentist. It is very vulgar to talk like a dentist when one isn't a dentist. It produces a false impression.

ALGERNON: Well, that is exactly what dentists always do. Now, go on! Tell me the whole thing. I may mention that I have always suspected you of being a confirmed and secret Bunburyist; and I am quite sure of it now.

QUESTION

The Importance of Being Earnest is generally regarded as a sparkling verbal drama. Discuss the extent to which, on the contrary, any production demands physical business and visual jokes.

This scene is from Act I, whilst Jack and Algy are still alone, awaiting the arrival for tea of Lady Bracknell and Gwendolen Fairfax. Its importance for the development of plot and character is that it establishes the habitual deceptions practised by the two men in the course of their everyday lives. It introduces the term 'Bunburyist' which Algy will shortly explain as being a convenient excuse for escaping social obligations; and it shows how the two young men differ from each other. Algy is clearly in control of this situation whilst Jack is chafing against his position but is unable to gain the upper hand. It therefore encapsulates their usual positions as they are played out in the rest of the action, where Jack is always trying to exert his influence, and is always failing – with Algy, as in this example, but also with Cecily, Gwendolen, and, of course, most significantly with Lady Bracknell in the rest of the play.

The scene is relatively unusual in the play as a whole because it involves a degree of physical humour, more in tune with slapstick or farce than with the sophisticated verbal comedy which appears as the play's keynote. The comedy arises from the mismatch between the appearance of two young men who look reasonably mature, and their behaviour, which is frankly schoolboyish. By holding onto the cigarette case, Algy maintains a physical superiority over Jack, which is mirrored also in his verbal advantage. Algy's sleight of hand which prevents Jack from getting hold of the cigarette case is thus a visual equivalent of his repartee. The importance of the physical moves is signalled by the relative abundance of stage directions which are much more sparse elsewhere in the play.

Along with the physical humour of this short passage, there is also the verbal humour common in the rest of the play. This involves a kind of **dramatic irony** in that Algy knows something that Jack does not know; and whilst the audience does not know the detail in this case, we are nonetheless aware of Jack's discomfiture which builds as Algy delays the final revelation of the complete inscription in the cigarette case, reading it a little at a time to heighten the suspense. It is a kind of comic torture, emphasised by the fact that Jack ought to know what has been inscribed in his own possession, but appears to have forgotten it. The contortions Jack goes through to avoid revealing the real identity of Little Cecily are counterpointed against Algy's poise because he knows that his friend is lying to him. The language of this exchange points out the farcical tone of the play as a whole, with Jack absurdly trying to argue that Aunts may be any size when the existence of Aunt Cecily is a patent fabrication, and insisting that his name is Jack, not Ernest, against everything that he has always told Algy.

Algy, of course, is having none of it. He points to Jack's card as evidence that his name is really Ernest.

He also insists that Jack's appearance naturally makes Ernest an appropriate name because he is 'the most earnest-looking person I ever saw in my life' (p. 257). This pun on a proper name which runs through the whole play is signalled here for the first time. A proper name, one might assume, has no concrete relationship with the character of the person who bears the name. There is no reason to assume, then, that a person whose name is Ernest has the qualities of earnestness – of a sincere and serious disposition – particularly as other characters have names which don't suit them. Algernon, for example, literally means 'moustached' though there is no evidence in the play that he has any facial hair; Laetitia (Miss Prism's christian name) inappropriately means 'joy'; Cecily comes from a Latin route that literally means 'blind' despite her knowingness; and Gwendolen derives from a Welsh word meaning 'white'. None of these names is especially appropriate to the characters who bear them, though Lady Bracknell's christian name, Augusta, is perfectly descriptive of her character.

This brief exchange, then, prefigures the ideals of Gwendolen and Cecily who both fall in love with the name of Ernest because it presumably suggests attractive masculine qualities to them, in particular a serious manner which they find strangely attractive. But it also prefigures the dénouement of the play as a whole, where Jack, who has denied the name of Ernest here, is discovered really to be called Ernest, a name which suits him despite all his deceptions; after all, he is not especially good at deceiving people and is far too serious in his disposition to enjoy Bunburying as Algy does.

The exchange also points to a significant difference between the two male leads. Shortly after this passage, Algy will tell us with pride of his invention of the invalid character of Bunbury who enables him

CONTEXT

Throughout the play, written evidence of a variety of kinds is shown to be fictitious. The name on Jack's card is wrong; the words Cecily and Gwendolen write in their diaries bears no relation to reality. Lady Bracknell has known some 'strange errors' (p. 304) in the Court Guides. Although this is a running joke throughout the play, it also raises the important philosophical question of what constitutes evidence for knowledge – what philosophers call an 'epistemological' question.

to do as he pleases despite Aunt Augusta's exacting social schedule. Algy is proud of his deceit; so proud that he is happy to share it with his friend, and to offer it as an important piece of advice for surviving marriage. Jack, however, is afraid of being discovered in deceit. He is more pompous than Algy, and has a stronger sense that appearance and reality ought to match. He believes in respectability and hates the idea of being caught out, hence the desperation of his lies about his little aunt who lives in Tunbridge Wells.

QUESTION
Discuss the ways in which Wilde's *The Importance of Being Earnest* constructs its characters. To what extent is characterization an issue of surface rather than depth?

This is, of course, a highly **ironic** position for him to find himself in. He is a man who believes in seriousness, and who knows that a gentleman should always tell the truth, but he ends up telling hilarious falsehoods which, in fact, deceive no one.

Algy, however, simply does not care about being caught out. That is just a part of the game that he sees life as being. Algy makes no pretence at having any moral position; and because this is a comic world, he is a character who suffers very little from the consequences of his own actions. It is Algy's amoral stance which takes precedence in the tone and incidents of the play. This is an anti-**realist** position in the play, since consequences are traditionally supposed to be what matters about action. Here, however, the audience is invited to laugh at the qualities of 'earnestness'; Jack/Ernest is the butt of the joke precisely because he believes that actions have consequences, and that the consequences are important. The play resolutely suggests otherwise.

TEXT 2 – ACT II (PP. 292–4)

GWENDOLEN AND CECILY FIGHT IT OUT FOR THE LOVE OF ERNEST

GWENDOLEN: Do you allude to me, Miss Cardew, as an entanglement? You are presumptuous. On an occasion of this kind it becomes more than a moral duty to speak one's mind. It becomes a pleasure.

CECILY: Do you suggest, Miss Fairfax, that I entrapped Ernest into an engagement? How dare you? This is no time for wearing the shallow mask of manners. When I see a spade I call it a spade.

GWENDOLEN [*satirically*]: I am glad to say that I have never seen a spade. It is obvious that our social spheres have been widely different.

[*Enter* MERRIMAN, *followed by the footman. He carries a salver, table cloth and plate stand.* CECILY *is about to retort. The presence of the servants exercises a restraining influence, under which both girls chafe.*]

MERRIMAN: Shall I lay tea here as usual, Miss?

CECILY [*sternly, in a calm voice*]: Yes, as usual. [MERRIMAN *begins to clear table and lay cloth. A long pause.* CECILY *and* GWENDOLEN *glare at each other.*]

GWENDOLEN: Are there many interesting walks in the vicinity, Miss Cardew?

CECILY: Oh! yes! a great many. From the top of one of the hills quite close one can see five counties.

GWENDOLEN: Five counties! I don't think I should like that; I hate crowds.

CECILY [*sweetly*]: I suppose that is why you live in town? [GWENDOLEN *bites her lip, and beats her foot nervously with her parasol.*]

GWENDOLEN [*looking round*]: Quite a well-kept garden this is, Miss Cardew.

CECILY: So glad you like it, Miss Fairfax.

GWENDOLEN: I had no idea there were any flowers in the country.

CECILY: Oh, flowers are as common here, Miss Fairfax, as people are in London.

GWENDOLEN: Personally I cannot understand how anybody manages to exist in the country, if anybody who is anybody does. The country always bores me to death.

CHECK THE BOOK

Regenia Gagnier in *Idylls of the Marketplace: Oscar Wilde and the Victorian Public* (1987) suggests that the characters in the play are 'mannequins' or puppets 'fixed in their masks' (p. 114). This may be one occasion when the mask of manners, as Cecily calls it, very nearly slips.

CECILY: Ah! this is what the newspapers call agricultural depression, is it not? I believe the aristocracy are suffering very much from it just at present. It is almost an epidemic amongst them, I have been told. May I offer you some tea, Miss Fairfax?

GWENDOLEN [*with elaborate politeness*]: Thank you. [*Aside.*] Detestable girl! But I require tea.

CECILY [*sweetly*]: Sugar?

GWENDOLEN [*superciliously*]: No, thank you. Sugar is not fashionable any more. [CECILY *looks angrily at her, takes up the tongs and puts four lumps of sugar into the cup.*]

CECILY [*severely*]: Cake or bread and butter?

GWENDOLEN [*in a bored manner*]: Bread and butter, please. Cake is rarely seen at the best houses nowadays.

CECILY [*cuts a very large slice of cake and puts it on the tray*]: Hand that to Miss Fairfax.

[MERRIMAN *does so, and goes out with footman.* GWENDOLEN *drinks the tea and makes a grimace. Puts down cup at once, reaches out her hand to the bread and butter, looks at it, and finds it is cake. Rises in indignation.*]

GWENDOLEN: You have filled my tea with lumps of sugar, and though I asked most distinctly for bread and butter, you have given me cake. I am known for the gentleness of my disposition, and the extraordinary sweetness of my nature, but I warn you, Miss Cardew, you may go too far.

CECILY [*rising*]: To save my poor, innocent, trusting boy from the machinations of any other girl there are no lengths to which I would not go.

GWENDOLEN: From the moment I saw you I distrusted you. I felt that you were false and deceitful. I am never deceived in such matters. My first impressions of people are invariably right.

CONTEXT

The use of forenames was eschewed in polite society – it was the *family* name that mattered – and even people who were quite close to each other as friends might continue to address each other formally. It is a striking fact that Jack and Algy call each other by their forenames from the outset of the play. A more usual form of address between men who were peers would be to address each other by their family names as Worthing and Moncrieff. It suggests a very great intimacy between the two men, one which might retrospectively come to be read as suggestive of a relationship that is more than mere friendship.

CECILY: It seems to me, Miss Fairfax, that I am trespassing on your valuable time. No doubt you have many other calls of a similar character to make in the neighbourhood.

This exchange between Cecily and Gwendolen takes place towards the end of Act II. It follows initially friendly relations between the two women in which they have even condescended to call each other by their christian names, instead of the formal polite address of Miss Cardew and Miss Fairfax.

Their original cordiality has now broken down because they have discovered that they are each engaged to be married to Ernest Worthing, and they are now bitter rivals. The comedy of this exchange arises from the fact that, because the two women have been well-brought-up, and are practised members of polite society, they are unable explicitly to vent their spleen in self-evident insult. Rather, they are forced to insult each other indirectly, or **periphrastically**, talking around the subject, rather than expressing it directly. They are further restrained by the entrance of the servants. In the period in which the play is set, there were strict rules of conduct about how one behaved in front of the family's servants, expressed in the phrase *pas devant*, a contraction of the French phrase for 'not in front of the servants or children'. Merriman's entrance with the tea-things means that hostilities have to appear to be suspended. The veneer of politeness must be maintained. Any servant observing Cecily and Gwendolen's conversation and Cecily's actions, however, could scarcely be in doubt as to the true state of their emotions. One of the interesting staging decisions in this passage, therefore, is how Merriman and the silent footman respond to what they see and hear.

They have no explicit stage directions to tell them how to act beyond the mechanics of passing plates and cups. They may behave entirely impassively, as the ideal servant is supposed to do. Alternatively, they may enjoy the discomfiture of the two ladies in their hostile exchanges, and be barely able to suppress their merriment: the breakdown of formal polite conversation between the Gwendolen and Cecily would thus risk a more significant social breakdown, in the assumed proper relationships between servants and the upper classes. Before Merriman and the footman

CHECK THE FILM
It is very instructive to compare and contrast the staging of this scene in the two film versions of *Earnest*. Asquith's version is far more theatrically staged, with very overt responses from Merriman the Butler – he frankly relishes the scene played out before him. Parker's version is rather understated in comparison.

CHECK THE BOOK

Jonathan Dollimore, in *Sexual Dissidence: Augustine to Wilde, Freud to Foucault* comments in detail on this scene. He also notes that the joke on plain speaking (calling a spade a spade) was repeated by Wilde in a number of places: for example, he wrote in a letter, that the man who called a spade a spade 'should be condemned to use one'.

arrive, it is clear that Gwendolen and Cecily are preparing for a real battle. The 'shallow mask of manners' has slipped, with Gwendolen offering to speak her mind, and Cecily preparing to 'call a spade a spade'. To speak plainly, however, is to break up the social game-playing on which this society is based. To speak one's mind, or to call a spade a spade, would represent a failure of upper-class manners, and a slanging match, especially in front of the servants, would be most inappropriate.

With the entrance of Merriman, therefore, hostilities are almost suspended, at least on the surface. The formality and exaggerated good manners of the exchange between the two women is emphasised by repetition of the formal mode of address, Miss Fairfax, Miss Cardew, especially in the context of earlier exchanges where the two women called each other by their Christian names. The conversation is one in which nothing controversial or unconventional is mentioned. Gwendolen, for example, makes apparently anodyne remarks about walks in the neighbourhood, and the abundance of flowers in the well-kept garden. But only the surface is polite, as Gwendolen's nervous gesture with her parasol indicates. The two women will continue to score points off each other without breaking out into open insult. Surprisingly perhaps, it is probably Cecily, the rural innocent who wins this bout. When Gwendolen describes being able to see five counties as crowded, she is unsettled by Cecily's response that hating crowds is presumably why she lives in the town. Similarly, the innocence of a conventional remark about flowers provokes Cecily to describe flowers as being as common in the country 'as people are in London' – a barbed response which depends on the pun on 'common' which means both 'usual' and 'vulgar'.

The scene moves to its comic climax, however, in actions rather than words. The tea-table, a most formal space for 1890s culture, is reduced to a 'bun-fight'. Cecily is goaded by Gwendolen's snobbery as she notes that sugar is not fashionable, and that the best houses never serve cake; these are indirect but very pointed attacks on Cecily's own home. Cecily retaliates by making Gwendolen physically uncomfortable. Her tea is undrinkable because it has so much sugar in it; and she cannot eat cake without appearing unfashionable. This is a joke which presumably refers to Marie

Antoinette's famous exhortation to the French peasantry when she heard they had no bread: 'Let them eat cake'. It is a joke at the expense of Gwendolen's class position. Eating cake would make her 'common' since it is peasants who eat cake, and since cake is also 'unfashionable'. Her only response, once the servants have departed is to tackle Cecily head on by stating precisely what **solecisms** (breaches of etiquette) she has committed, which rather suggests that Gwendolen has lost the battle, since her pretence of manners collapses first.

Cecily, however, does not crumble. Her parting sally is a politely worded, though maliciously intended, invitation for Gwendolen to leave ('I am trespassing on your valuable time'), followed by the deeply cutting final shot: 'No doubt you have many other calls of a similar character to make in the neighbourhood'. Given that Gwendolen has come to the country in pursuit of her so-called fiancé, to suggest that she may have similar calls to make is deeply insulting. The conversation is cut short, however, by Jack's arrival, and the process of disentangling who is engaged to whom begins. This scene is very funny to the reader and the theatre audience, not only because of its content and tone, but also because of its context, and because of its play on the mismatch between appearance and reality. We seem to be watching two sweet young girls in conversation, but the content of what they say is at odds with both their class positions and with our expectations of them, derived from what we know of sweet young girls in comedies of manners. We know also, however, that no harm will be done. This is not a world in which insults are taken to heart, or where actions have serious consequences. Just one page later, the two women who have been metaphorically at each others' throats are suddenly prepared to call each other 'sister' (Act II, p. 295), as if they have forgotten this vicious exchange. What Cecily calls 'the shallow mask of manners' is very easily resumed. There is no psychological realism here. Cecily and Gwendolen do not resent the behaviour of the other in the long term. They suffer no distress. This reflects on the nature of Oscar Wilde's characters, who are all surface without substance. It also suggests that Cecily and Gwendolen will make very formidable wives; not for nothing is Gwendolen Lady Bracknell's daughter.

> **? QUESTION**
> The word repartee means literally the rapid exchange of blows in fencing. To what extent is it fair to read the verbal exchanges of *The Importance of Being Earnest* as 'battles'? Who, in your view, are the winners and losers of the various exchanges?

TEXT 3 – ACT I (PP. 267–9)

LADY BRACKNELL DISCOVERS JACK'S UNORTHODOX BACKGROUND

CONTEXT

The joke here on the 'purple of commerce' demands that audience understands the difference between a man who is born into a respectable family and one who is 'self-made' by his own efforts. To be born in the purple implies good breeding or blood. Commerce is the preserve of the self-made man. The purple of commerce is therefore a contradiction in terms. Additionally, one rises from the ranks of the poor, not from the aristocracy. As ever, the characters achieve their comic effects by the reversal of commonplace presumptions.

LADY BRACKNELL: … Now to minor matters. Are your parents living?

JACK: I have lost both my parents.

LADY BRACKNELL: To lose one parent, Mr Worthing, may be regarded as a misfortune; to lose both looks like carelessness. Who was your father? He was evidently a man of some wealth. Was he born in what the Radical papers call the purple of commerce, or did he rise from ranks of the aristocracy?

JACK: I am afraid I really don't know. The fact is, Lady Bracknell, I said I had lost my parents. It would be nearer the truth to say that my parents seem to have lost me … I don't actually know who I am by birth. I was … well, I was found.

LADY BRACKNELL: Found!

JACK: The late Mr Thomas Cardew, an old gentleman of a very charitable and kindly disposition, found me, and gave me the name of Worthing, because he happened to have a first-class ticket for Worthing in his pocket at the time. Worthing is a place in Sussex. It is a seaside resort.

LADY BRACKNELL: Where did the charitable gentleman who had a first-class ticket for this seaside resort find you?

JACK [*gravely*]: In a hand-bag.

LADY BRACKNELL: A hand-bag?

JACK [*very seriously*]: Yes, Lady Bracknell. I was in a hand-bag – a somewhat large, black, leather hand-bag, with handles to it – an ordinary hand-bag in fact.

LADY BRACKNELL: In what locality did this Mr James, or Thomas, Cardew come across this ordinary hand-bag?

JACK: In the cloak-room at Victoria Station. It was given to him in mistake for his own.

LADY BRACKNELL: The cloak-room at Victoria Station?

JACK: Yes. The Brighton Line.

LADY BRACKNELL: The line is immaterial. Mr Worthing, I confess I feel somewhat bewildered by what you have just told me. To be born, or at any rate bred, in a hand-bag, whether it had handles or not, seems to me to display a contempt for the ordinary decencies of family life that reminds one of the worst excesses of the French Revolution. And I presume you know what that unfortunate movement led to? As for the particular locality in which the hand-bag was found, a cloak-room at a railway station might serve to conceal a social indiscretion – has probably, indeed, been used for that purpose before now – but it could hardly be regarded as an assured basis for a recognized position in good society.

JACK: May I ask you then what you would advise me to do? I need hardly say I would do anything in the world to ensure Gwendolen's happiness.

LADY BRACKNELL: I would strongly advise you, Mr Worthing, to try and acquire some relations as soon as possible, and to make a definite effort to produce at any rate one parent, of either sex, before the season is quite over.

JACK: Well, I don't see how I could possibly manage to do that. I can produce the hand-bag at any moment. It is in my dressing-room at home. I really think that should satisfy you, Lady Bracknell.

LADY BRACKNELL: Me, sir! What has it to do with me? You can hardly imagine that I and Lord Bracknell would dream of allowing our only daughter – a girl brought up with the utmost care – to marry into a cloak-room, and form an alliance with a parcel. Good morning, Mr Worthing![LADY BRACKNELL *sweeps out in majestic indignation.*]

CHECK THE BOOK

As Sos Eltis comments, the comedy of this speech depends on the enormous logical leap made by Lady Bracknell – from a personal tragedy to the major event of history in the space of one sentence. See Eltis, *Revising Wilde: Society and Subversion in the Plays of Oscar Wilde.*

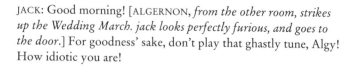

JACK: Good morning! [ALGERNON, *from the other room, strikes up the* Wedding March. *Jack looks perfectly furious, and goes to the door.*] For goodness' sake, don't play that ghastly tune, Algy! How idiotic you are!

This passage occurs towards the end of Act I. Jack has managed to propose to Gwendolen, and has been accepted by her. He now has to persuade her mother, Lady Bracknell, that he is an eligible bachelor. So far, the questions have gone well, and Lady Bracknell seems well-disposed to like Jack, not least because of his large fortune. She has not minded that he regards smoking as his occupation, that he is entirely ignorant and that he knows nothing of politics. These all seem admirable qualifications for her daughter's husband – and given the extent to which Gwendolen resembles her mother, her judgement is probably sound.

This passage charts the change that comes over Lady Bracknell's opinions when she discovers the 'minor matter' that Jack has no proper family connections. This is a famous and closely constructed comic scene which builds to a crescendo with Lady Bracknell's refusal to contemplate her daughter's 'alliance with a parcel'. The scene has become famous in part because of Anthony Asquith's 1953 film version, starring Edith Evans as Lady Bracknell. Evans's extremely exaggerated delivery of the line 'A hand-bag?' turned the question into an exclamation of outraged disgust, and many audiences regard this as the most important and famous line in the play. Evans played Lady Bracknell as an out-and-out battle-axe who brooked no dissension from her own points of view about propriety and respectability. More recent West-End performances, notably Judi Dench's 1982 portrayal of Lady Bracknell, have taken a rather different track. Dench was relatively young for a part traditionally played by older women. Dench went against tradition in almost swallowing the line 'A hand-bag?', and played the rest of the scene towards a crescendo on the line that describes Jack as a parcel. As Katharine Worth comments (in *Oscar Wilde*), Dench's playing of the role made Lady Bracknell appear more human.

The scene begins with a typical Bracknell inversion of the usual sense of a polite **euphemism**. To say that one has lost one's parents is, of course, to state **periphrastically** that they are dead. This mirrors Lady Bracknell's earlier strictures on Bunbury's health, as if

CHECK THE FILM

Judi Dench plays the role of Lady Bracknell in Parker's film version of the play in a reprise of her role from the 1982 stage version. A really interesting point of comparison between the two film versions is their treatment of Jack's interrogation by his potential mother-in-law. The two screenplays locate these scenes rather differently. And where Edith Evans elongated the words 'a hand-bag' to immense and comic length, Dench's Lady Bracknell is much more taken aback. Commentaries in the DVD version of Parker's film discuss the choices made in his version of this scene.

an invalid makes a moral choice about whether or not he is ill. Presumably if one's parents are dead, one cannot help it – it's not a matter of choice, and cannot therefore be seen as 'careless'. She must, of course, insist on knowing who the parents were. Even if Jack's personal qualities (or lack of them in traditional terms) are acceptable, bloodlines matter to the aristocrat in her. She wants to know whether Jack comes from a nouveau riche family, that is, a family who have made their own money in commerce; or from an aristocratic family, with inherited wealth and status. It does not actually matter to her which answer he produces, so long as his parents are respectable. Her questioning leads, of course, to Jack's farcical admission that he does not know who his parents were, that he is a foundling discovered in a hand-bag and adopted out of charity: he could be anyone.

> **CONTEXT**
>
> Wilde had made rather more serious use of this theme in his earlier play, *A Woman of No Importance* (1893), in which the woman of the title is the abandoned mistress of Lord Illingworth, and her son is the illegitimate child of that liaison.

For audiences used to **melodramas** on the 1890s stage, that Jack is a foundling sets up certain generic expectations. In an age before easy divorce, and when illegitimacy was a profound social stigma, the foundling child was traditionally presented in the tragic mode, an outcast whose existence is the sad result of an illicit sexual relationship. (This is the force of the joke in Act III, when Jack wrongly identifies Miss Prism as his 'Mother!', and makes a sentimental speech straight from melodrama about the sexual double standard which condones male sexual irregularity, but punishes the woman and her illegitimate child.)

Because he is a foundling, then, Lady Bracknell assumes that he must be the result of 'a social indiscretion'. His fortune cannot rescue him from his illegitimacy, and he is immediately placed beyond the pale of respectability. Her shock that he should want to marry her daughter despite his lack of family builds slowly to a climax through the scene. Depending on the way that the scene is played, Lady Bracknell might be seen as nonplussed or entirely in control of the situation; either interpretation is possible, but the reader/spectator should think about what the effect of Lady Bracknell losing control would be on the stage; and, again, about how the scene works if she is seen as torturing Jack with the inadequacy of his background. In either case, she teases an explanation out of Jack in slow and painful stages. The speech in which Jack introduces his benefactor, Mr Thomas Cardew, we must assume is spoken very slowly. Jack pauses between sentences to await Lady Bracknell's response, which is not forthcoming. He, being a polite young man, cannot let a gap in the conversation develop, and he therefore adds detail to detail to prevent a silence from developing. Lady Bracknell may not have a very practical attitude to life, but she probably knows that Worthing is in Sussex without Jack telling her. That he produces **phatic** speech is a symptom of his nervousness.

The pace is also slowed down because of the way that Lady Bracknell phrases her questions, repeating information that Jack has just given her as part of her move to get the next piece of information. Moreover, she stops being punctiliously polite as the scene progresses, getting Thomas Cardew's name wrong, for example, which suggests that either she wasn't listening properly, or that she doesn't care about Jack's answer. He squirms, whilst she becomes increasingly indifferent to the outcome of the conversation. With her exclamation of the word 'Found!', she has, after all, come to realise that Jack is not, after all, a very eligible young man. The absurdity of the situation is compounded when Lady Bracknell takes off in a flight of fury about the impossibility of Jack as a prospective son-in-law. With no family he has no hope. But what his situation has to do with the French Revolution is not at all clear. Lady Bracknell become carried away with her own eloquence, and moves into **hyperbole**, meaning overstatement, and the precise opposite of good manners. To describe Jack's existence (even if she does so only implicitly) as a 'social indiscretion' is deeply insulting. But if Jack has no family connections, he has no assured social position, and Lady Bracknell need not keep up the pretence of politeness, hence her parting shot that Jack's family is a cloak-room and that he himself is a parcel.

As Lady Bracknell sweeps from the room, Algy strikes up the Wedding March on his piano, his second musical intervention, which underscores the triviality of what has just passed in his rooms. The music could scarcely be less appropriate for the immediate context; and yet, the curtain will eventually come down on three engaged couples. Algy is irrepressibly optimistic, and as the play will show, he is right to be so. Lady Bracknell's apparently final say on the subject will be shown to be anything but final. No single action or speech functions beyond itself, or leads to irreparable consequences.

PART THREE

CRITICAL APPROACHES

CHARACTERISATION

This section contains a brief description of each of the characters in order of their appearance, followed by a discussion of Oscar Wilde's use of character in the play, and its implications.

LANE

Lane is Algernon Moncrieff's butler. We first see him arranging the tea-table in Algy's rooms, whilst Algy is offstage playing the piano. Whilst this is a minor role, Lane is important in the establishment of the tone of the play. His relationship with Algy is apparently one of deference and politeness – the classic master–servant relationship.

This appearance, however, is belied by his exchanges with Algy in which he discusses champagne-consumption in bachelor establishments, and the 'demoralising' effects of marriage, including his own, which was the result not of romantic attachment but of a 'misunderstanding between myself and a young person' (Act I, p. 253). This seems like a very slight exchange, but given that the play is about deception in the service of romantic love, his view that a marriage might be based on misunderstanding rather than on love is a deft signal of one of the themes that the play explores. Again, at the end of Act I, as he hands Algy sherry and receives orders to prepare his clothes for Bunburying, Algy hopes for a fine day for his adventure:

ALGERNON: I hope tomorrow will be a fine day,

LANE: It never is, sir.

ALGERNON: Lane, you're a perfect pessimist.

LANE: I do my best to give satisfaction, sir. (Act I, p. 273)

A conventionally polite remark about the weather is given a different status by Lane's reply. The kind of satisfaction that Lane provides is to give perfect service whilst **ironising** the conventional power relationships between master and servant: Lane is Algy's

CONTEXT

It is noticeable in the play that none of the servants is given a forename. It was common throughout the Victorian period for servants – both male and female – to be addressed by their surnames alone. There is also ample evidence (for instance in *The Diaries of Hannah Cullwick*, a serving maid) that masters and mistresses often used merely generic names for their servants, calling all the maids 'Mary' for instance, no matter what their real names were.

conversation equal, if not his social peer. For most of Act I, Lane's role is confined to showing people in and out, and in serving tea or drinks. He is a very reliable servant, demonstrated when he excuses the lack of cucumber sandwiches for Lady Bracknell on his own initiative, but he is not a servile servant.

ALGERNON MONCRIEFF

Algernon Moncrieff, usually called Algy, is one of the play's major characters, on-stage for much of the action. It is clear that he is an idle young man, prone to boredom – it is because he gets bored in the city that he has invented his imaginary friend, Bunbury, in order to have a ready excuse to leave whenever he pleases. He has no visible means of support: as Lady Bracknell comments, 'He has nothing, but he looks everything' (Act III, p. 306), and he lives entirely for his own pleasure. For him, life is a game with elaborate but inconsequential rules. His only passions are for food and drink and for clothes. It is a standing joke in the play that Algy is always eating, from the cucumber sandwiches and the dinner he forces from Jack in Act I, to the lunch he cadges from Cecily in Act II, to the muffins with which Act II ends. One of Algy's objections to Jack is that Jack is not nearly serious enough about food. His other objection is that Jack dresses badly. Algy observes that he has never known anyone to take so much time dressing for so little effect, and that Jack is the last person to whom he would entrust the choice of his own clothing. He is a dandy figure, and as such, would have been read as effeminate by Oscar Wilde's contemporary audiences who regarded attention to dress as a feminine attribute.

CHECK THE BOOK
Ellen Moers' *The Dandy: Brummell to Beerbohm* provides a helpful history of the dandy figure in nineteenth-century literature and art.

Algy's is a life of deceit. He lives the life of an upper-class man, but without the income to support it (in Act I we see him tearing up his bills, not paying them, and in the four-act version of the play, he is nearly arrested for debt). He lies almost all the time: about Bunbury, about sandwiches, about his own identity when he disguises himself as Ernest. His lies, like his greed, however, are not supposed to be read as serious moral failings. The world of the play is one which takes nothing seriously (remember the subtitle, *A Trivial Comedy for Serious People*), and Algy is the primary site of moral reversals. At the end of the play, he is not punished for deceit, but rewarded for it with Cecily's hand in marriage. His function in the play is therefore to represent an amoral world where transgression is rewarded, not punished, and where the usual values are reversed. His foibles provoke laughter, not outrage.

JACK WORTHING

Jack Worthing (known as Jack in the country and as Ernest in town) appears a very similar character to Algy. Jack is also idle – though he appears to have the income to support his lifestyle. Like his friend, he is leading a double life of deceit: he is respectable in the country, rakish and dissolute in the city, under the covering identity of his fictitious brother Ernest. There are, nonetheless, important differences between them. Jack appears to be a more sincere character, and his deceits are rather less successful than those of Algy – Act I, for example, has Jack being 'found out' via the means of his cigarette case; Algy is most unlikely to be caught out like that. Jack is also less dandified, less greedy and a less accomplished liar than Algy. It is on Jack that much of the play's comedy is played out. He does not win verbal sparring matches – with Algy, with Gwendolen, with Lady Bracknell, or even with Cecily. He usually does as he is told, and the eventual revelation of his true identity should come as no real surprise to the reader/spectator, nor to the other characters in the play.

Ernest is a name which suggests truthfulness and sincerity. In this world, these are attributes which make one easily manipulated, which is presumably why Gwendolen finds Jack so attractive as a possible husband – she likes the idea of a husband who can be kept under her thumb. Algy, Gwendolen and Cecily are all easily able to make Jack do what they want him to. Jack plays the role of the play's **ingenue**, the innocent-abroad character, manipulated by circumstances and other characters, a part one might more usually expect to be given to the young female lead in the general run of the **comedy of manners**.

A significant fact in Jack's existence is that he does not know who he is, having been abandoned in a hand-bag at a railway station as a small baby, twenty-eight years before the current action. In interpreting his place in the play, it is probably important to remember that he has been left in the hand-bag having been mistaken for a three-volume novel. The play's interest in the relationship between truth and fiction is woven into this plot device.

> **? QUESTION**
> The major characters of *Earnest* are 'paired' – two young men and two young women, who are compared and contrasted with each other. Discuss the points of comparison and contrast between the two pairs and consider the effectiveness of this device in Wilde's play.

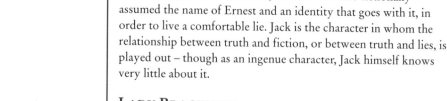

A man whose name is really Ernest, implying truth and sincerity, has been mistaken for a fiction; this man has also fictionally assumed the name of Ernest and an identity that goes with it, in order to live a comfortable lie. Jack is the character in whom the relationship between truth and fiction, or between truth and lies, is played out – though as an ingenue character, Jack himself knows very little about it.

LADY BRACKNELL

CHECK THE FILM
Oliver Parker's film version of the play implies that not only did Lady Bracknell marry without a fortune any kind, but that she inveigled her husband into marriage after a successful (but highly disreputable) career on the music-hall stage, from where she seduced him.

Lady Bracknell's function in the drama is pivotal. She is the prime reason for the plot's complications. For example, if she were to agree to the marriage of Gwendolen and Jack, there would be no plot at all; and Algy has invented Bunbury – another source of complication – precisely in order to escape from her and the social obligations she imposes on him. Nonetheless, she is also a comic figure. A **stock character** from the **comedy of manners** is the older woman who wields power, but is regarded by the audience (if not the other characters) as comic because her days of sexual attractiveness are over. This is Lady Bracknell's role. She is unmotivated except by the pleasure that she takes in power. Given her own background of relative social obscurity ('When I married Lord Bracknell I had no fortune of any kind. But I never dreamed for a moment of allowing that to stand in my way' – Act III, p. 305), there is no logic in her objection to Jack's marriage to Gwendolen, particularly given the size of his fortune, and his 'suitability' in other areas.

That she has no motive except power is important for our understanding of the play's **genre**. This is not a psychological drama in which hidden motivations need to be sought as explanations for action. The action here is so inconsequential that it requires no explanation whatever.

GWENDOLEN FAIRFAX

Gwendolen Fairfax is Lady Bracknell's daughter and the object of Jack Worthing's affections. She is a young attractive woman who is eminently marriageable, despite her resemblance to her formidable mother; she will clearly grow more and more like her as the years go by. She is chafing under the tight control over her life that is exercised by Lady Bracknell, imaged in her minor acts of disobedience to her mother, such as her refusal to leave the room or her reluctance to go to the carriage in Act I, or her flight to Jack's country house in Act II.

The difference between men and women in the play is one of social freedom; the men are able to make alternative lives for themselves, but Gwendolen is closely chaperoned, and is seldom able to escape. Like the two men, Gwendolen leads an idle life, made up of socialising, paying visits and involving herself in minor cultural events. Also, like Algy, she is very cynical about social life, and a very accomplished performer on the social scene. It is clear that her projected marriage to Jack will see him as a hen-pecked husband, just as we may assume that her unseen father, Lord Bracknell, is ruled by his wife. Gwendolen dramatises the extent to which this is a world without serious principles, her only ideal being that her husband must bear the name of Ernest. Even romantic love, traditionally a serious motivation, even in comedy, is an insincere performance in this play.

MISS PRISM

Miss Prism is Cecily's governess at Jack's house in the country. As such, her position is that of a social anomaly in that her status is greater than that of an ordinary servant, but less than that of a member of her employer's family. On the other hand, in other works of nineteenth-century literature (notably Charlotte Brontë's *Jane Eyre*, 1847, and Anne Brontë's *Agnes Grey*, 1847) the governess's unstable social position was treated as potentially tragic. The governess was generally a middle-class woman whose class status was called into question by the fact that she had to earn her own living instead of being supported financially by either her husband or her father. On the other hand, whilst teaching as a governess in a private home was a low-paid occupation, it was at least respectable.

In this context, however, Miss Prism is a comic figure blissfully unaware of her own comic potential. Like Lady Bracknell, she is past the age when women have traditionally been viewed as sexually attractive: as Lady Bracknell puts it, Miss Prism is 'a female of repellent aspect, remotely connected with education' (Act III, p. 308) – a cruel but accurate description. Unlike Lady Bracknell, however, Miss Prism

CHECK THE FILM
Again, in the Oliver Parker film, the screenplay signals her rebellion against her mother much more strongly. For example she meets Ernest in a public house (actually an utter anachronism for the 1890s when no respectable woman of her class could have entered such an establishment); and she signals her devotion to Ernest as well as her revolt against her mother by the very 1990s strategy of having Ernest's name tattooed on her buttock. These moments in the film, of course, tell us more about the 1990s than the 1890s.

The governess
question had been
discussed with
remarkable
regularity (given
the relatively small
numbers of
women involved in
the profession)
from the mid-
century onwards.
The often under-
educated middle-
class women who
took up the
profession were,
in the 1840s and
1850s, usually
regarded as victims
of the social
system. By the
1890s, however,
as Miss Prism's
presentation
implies, the panic
about governesses
was more or less
over, and the
figure of the
governess was less
common in both
reality and fiction.
Nonetheless, one
further important
version of the
governess post-
dates *Earnest* in
Henry James's
ghost story and
psychological
thriller, *The Turn of
the Screw* (1899).

lacks social power, hence her comically desperate attempts to persuade Canon Chasuble into marriage as a way of escaping her marginal social status. She is also a modified version of the **stock character** of the sexually voracious older woman to be found in the **comedy of manners** and other modes of eighteenth-century fiction. Here, though, the comedy comes not so much from the actual pursuit of Canon Chasuble, which is sedate if desperate, but from the fact she cannot break the bounds of propriety to speak her desires in so many words. There is a mismatch between appearance and reality, and between language and the realities it is supposed to express.

Miss Prism's name is important too. In physics, a prism is an object which separates white light into the constituent colours of the rainbow. One assumes that Miss Prism is dowdy rather than well-dressed, so that there is a comedy even in her name. Add to that the possibility that Miss Prism is a near pun on 'misprision', meaning 'misunderstanding', and one can see that Lady Bracknell is more accurate than perhaps she intends when she says that the governess is only 'remotely connected with education'. Her use of language, and in particular her coinage of the **neologism** 'womanthrope' (Act II, p. 279), implies that her own education is scarcely adequate to the task of teaching Cecily.

She is also profoundly narrow-minded, moralistic and old-fashioned. Her attitude to the 'wickedness' of Ernest is un-Christian and unforgiving, and the novel that she wrote in which 'the good ended happily, and the bad ended unhappily' (Act II, p. 275) is suitable only for the circulating libraries – it is not a work of high literature with complex moral values. She is so concerned with respectability that she even tells Cecily to leave out a chapter on the fall of the rupee in her political economy as unsuitable for a young girl to read unchaperoned: 'It is too sensational. Even these metallic problems have their melodramatic side' (Act II, p. 276). She is a prude who does not really know the proper limits of prudery.

Despite the fact that she is generally ineffectual, however, Miss Prism's role in the play's plot is also important. It is she who is ultimately responsible for Jack Worthing's having been discovered in hand-bag when she mixes up her novel and the baby in her care twenty-eight years before the action begins. Her fortuitous presence in Jack's household is too much of a coincidence to be viewed in any sense realistically: Miss Prism's role is to pile on the comedic grotesquerie of the absurd world which Oscar Wilde has created. The coincidence for which she is responsible, along with her absurd three-volume novel, constitute Oscar Wilde's attack on the Victorian tradition of **realism** in fiction and drama, in which literary texts were supposed to be accurate reflections of real life, to encompass complex moral problems, and to be based on a belief in cause and effect in narrative lines rather than coincidence.

CECILY CARDEW

Cecily Cardew, Jack's ward, and Gwendolen's rival for 'Ernest Worthing' appears at first to be the female **ingenue** character – that is, the innocent abroad. She is the youngest member of the cast at eighteen, regarded as a marriageable age by contemporary society. She is clearly pretty, but her appearance does not have the gloss of Gwendolen's city-made attire. As Lady Bracknell comments: 'Pretty child! your dress is sadly simple, and your hair seems almost as Nature might have left it' (Act III, p. 304).

At first sight, both to Lady Bracknell, and to the audience, Cecily has social possibilities because she is rich and pretty. We also see her, however, as a young woman with pronounced characteristics of her own. She pays no attention to her lessons, has 'a capital appetite' (Act I, p. 271) (which may be why Algy is attracted to her even before they meet) and a swift intelligence for picking up the niceties of social situations. When we first meet her, she appears innocent, but she is already scheming to achieve what she wants – not to do her lessons, to meet Algy in the guise of Ernest. In her hostile exchanges with Gwendolen in Act II, she is Gwendolen's equal in **repartee** despite her limited experience.

Like Algy and Gwendolen, Cecily resists seriousness, seeing it as both silly and unattractive, commenting to Miss Prism, for example, that German is an unbecoming language, and that German lessons make her plain (Act II, p. 274), and refusing to interpret her uncle's mourning clothes with the gravity which they are supposed to signify. For all her apparent simplicity, she is a highly manipulative character; and we must assume that in her life beyond the end of the play, she will continue to learn how to get what she wants,

CHECK THE FILM
The contrast between the dress of Cecily and Gwendolen in Oliver Parker's film of *Earnest* is very marked indeed. Gwendolen wears the clothes of the fashionable urban sophisticate; Cecily dresses in the manner of a Pre-Raphaelite damsel. (The Pre-Raphaelites were a Victorian art movement, interested in representations of Medieval scenes and stories.) Throughout the film, she fantasises that she is the heroine of a poem by Tennyson (for instance, 'The Lady of Shalott', 1841), about to be rescued by Algy as a highly unlikely knight in shining armour.

following Gwendolen's example. Algy will also be a hen-pecked husband in the world beyond the end of the play.

CANON CHASUBLE

Canon Chasuble is the local rector in the parish which contains Jack's country house. He is a relatively high-ranking churchman, with his title of Canon which means that he has a role in the bishop's office.

That he is a high-ranking clergyman suggests that Oscar Wilde is **satirising** the Church of England, since, like Miss Prism, Canon Chasuble is extremely ineffectual. His sermons have had no effect on the local population who continue to produce children with alarming regularity, which is not surprising since he tends to reproduce the same sermon for every occasion, implying the utter uselessness of his words:

> My sermon on the meaning of the manna in the wilderness can be adapted to almost any occasion, joyful, or, as in the present case, distressing … I have preached it at harvest celebrations, christenings, confirmations, on days of humiliation and festal days. The last time I delivered it was in the Cathedral, as a charity sermon on behalf of the Society for the Prevention of Discontent among the Upper Orders. The Bishop, who was present, was much struck by some of the analogies I drew. (Act II, pp. 280–1)

And, as Cecily notes: 'Dr Chasuble is a most learned man. He has never written a single book, so you can imagine how much he knows' (Act II, p. 289).

The canon appears in the play for a satiric purpose. He enables Oscar Wilde to poke fun at the established church, thus emphasising the theme of treating serious things trivially. He is not a man of firm purpose or principle, as one might expect a clergyman to be. He enters the play arguing with Miss Prism about the value of celibacy in the priesthood, trying to put her off her pursuit of him. At the end of the play, however, he capitulates, and grasps her in his arms to make a third couple in the play's final tableau. He is a bumbler who trips through life untouched by its events. As such, he is the only future husband in the play not to be pitied. If Cecily and Gwendolen are likely to turn into Lady Bracknell's doubles with maturity, Miss Prism is already mature and fixed, and his marriage will at least prevent him from being attractive to other ladies of the parish by placing him out of the way of temptation.

MERRIMAN

Merriman is Jack's butler in the country, and is therefore the rural equivalent of Lane in Act I. He has less to do than Lane, though he is present during Gwendolen and Cecily's tea-party, and his presence, along with that of other servants, puts a brake on their hostilities. An interesting staging point would be in how he responds to that scene, though he has no words to say.

Like Lane, Merriman is a good servant. He warns the courting couples, for example, of the arrival of Lady Bracknell with a timely cough. Apart from these two incidents, his role is confined to showing people in and out, and obeying incidental orders. His is a far more traditional role than Lane's – he is not cheeky and he in no way disrupts the social order. Perhaps the countryside is a more innocent space that the city, and in the country, the servants are shown to know their place, in comparison to the urban sophistication implied by the Algy and Gwendolen's way of life, and by Algy's more free and easy relationship with Lane.

OSCAR WILDE'S USE OF CHARACTERISATION

From the descriptions above, it soon becomes clear that Oscar Wilde's characters in this play are not quite what one might expect. There is patterning and balance in characterisation rather than the expression of deep psychological motives. These are characters that exist entirely on the surface; psychology and motivation are scarcely appropriate words to describe them.

The balance achieved by the pairings of Jack and Algy, and of Gwendolen and Cecily immediately suggests that this is in no sense a **realist** or **naturalist** drama. It is far more like the artificial world of puppetry than the usually naturalist world of the Victorian stage. Indeed, throughout his writings, Oscar Wilde very seldom used the word character at all, preferring to describe himself and his fictional creations as 'personalities'.

> **CONTEXT**
>
> 'It is only the superficial qualities that last. Man's deeper nature is soon found out', wrote Wilde in his 'Phrases and Philosophies for the Use of the Young'.

In late-Victorian England, character was a very important word, even beyond literature. One would describe a person of whom one approved as 'having character', meaning that this was a person who could be trusted, whose external appearance and internal morality were in accordance with each other. Oscar Wilde had been a Greek scholar, and he knew quite well that the word character derived from the Greek, meaning 'something imprinted, distinctive nature of the thing'. Character was supposed to go right through a person, like lettering in a stick of rock. Moreover, it was supposed also to be a unique marker – each person's character is unique and individual; no one person can be quite like any other in this understanding of the term.

CHECK THE BOOK

This idea is developed further in Ruth Robbins's essay, 'Judas always writes the biography: the Many Lives of Oscar Wilde' in Ruth Robbins and Julian Wolfreys, eds, *Victorian Identities* (1995).

Personality, however, derives from the Latin word 'persona', meaning in the first instance 'actor's mask'. Personality, that is, is a kind of disguise. It is, for example, the face that one shows to the social world as opposed to one's 'real' self. Society demands conformity and regularity – there are rules of proper social behaviour, and the rules may well often be at odds with what one really wants to do. To get on in society, Oscar Wilde's play seems to argue, you have to be able to *act your part well*; your acting ability is what you are judged on, and this ability is very likely to have nothing at all to do with whether you are really a good person or not.

As one reads or watches *The Importance of Being Earnest*, it becomes clear that Jack is very nearly interchangeable with Algy, and that Gwendolen and Cecily are virtual clones of each other. The two women both keep a diary in which they record patently fabricated events, they both dream of marrying a man called Ernest, and, of course, they call each other 'sister' when they discover the deception that has been practised on them over the existence of Ernest Worthing. The two men appropriate the same fictitious identity as Ernest Worthing; and they too are very alike, at least in the surface of their lives. There is no sense in *The Importance of Being Earnest* in which character could be described in terms of uniqueness and individuality. The figures that populate the play are personalities in Oscar Wilde's terms, not characters. This idea of characterisation is one of the sources of the play's social satire. Good society is no guarantee here of goodness in the people who inhabit it. Furthermore, in this version of character, Oscar Wilde also attacks the ideals of romantic love. If, after all, the lovers are interchangeable, the ideal of falling in love with a particular individual is clearly overthrown. The pairings are not a matter of choice or instinct towards a unique beloved. In this avowedly artificial structure, Oscar Wilde is showing us that the ideal of romantic love is itself artificial, a social construction – perhaps even a game.

PLOT

There is a very strong sense as one reads or watches the play that the plot is quite possibly the least important thing about *The Importance of Being Earnest*. The story the play dramatises is very slight indeed, and is so unlikely as to appear absurd; much of its action points to the genre of farce. Certainly no audience is really interested in the psychological motivations of the characters, nor in the resolution of the 'mystery' of Jack's parentage: moreover, the resolutions of the romantic plots in engagements at the end of the play are entirely predictable. The audience is never motivated by an urge to know 'what happens next'. Rather we watch stylised actions and conversations, performed by stylised characters who require no audience sympathy or empathy. Thus whilst one could produce an accurate description of the plotting strategies which discussed the significance of 'identity' as a major theme of the play, such a response would not reflect the spirit of a play whose actions are gloriously inconsequential. As Oscar Wilde wrote in his 'Phrases and Philosophies for the Use of the Young' (1894), 'Nothing that actually occurs is of the smallest importance', an accurate description of the structure of the play.

This not to say, however, that the plot is not closely structured. It is in fact very meticulously planned, with many apparently throwaway lines which prefigure later action. The most significant examples are Algy's eavesdropping on Gwendolen and Jack's hurried conversation in his rooms at Half-Moon Street, which gives him Jack's country address and thus the means for his next bunburying expedition; and Miss Prism's tiny remark about having once written a 'three-volume novel' which we later learn she has mistaken for the baby who turns out to be Jack. Although the impression of the whole play is that it is light and frothy, with little substance, there is very little dialogue which does not 'tell' in some way. The point is that the

 CHECK THE BOOK

Kerry Powell's *Oscar Wilde and the Theatre of the 1890s* establishes the extent to which Wilde's play, far from being original, reprises a series of stock situations from contemporary farces on the West End stage. In particular, he demonstrates that a number of significant plot elements are derived from an unpublished play entitled *The Foundling*, by W. Lestcocq and E. M. Robson that had been produced in 1894.

'telling' is rather more about atmosphere than action. Oscar Wilde has moved the traditional emphasis in plotting away from **suspense** and towards manner or style. You do not approach the play in order to find out whether Jack will marry Gwendolen in the end, since given the tone of the play, it is perfectly obvious that he will; one approaches the play to enjoy the way in which the resolution is achieved – the fact that it will be achieved is never in any doubt.

LANGUAGE AND STYLE

CHECK THE BOOK

Wilde himself was a renowned speaker and conversationalist. As Richard Ellmann notes in his biography of the playwright, *Oscar Wilde*, even the poet W. B. Yeats was extremely impressed by Wilde's conversational style, recording in his *Autobiographies* that Wilde spoke perfect sentences, as if he had been rehearsing them all night.

Even allowing for quite significant shifts in the ways in which people express themselves in the century since *The Importance of Being Earnest* was first performed, no-one has ever spoken in quite the way that Oscar Wilde's characters speak.

The style of their language is markedly artificial. Because in the polite society of the period, one was not supposed to express one's deepest feelings in public, or even to say anything mildly controversial, the language of social intercourse in mixed-sex groups in the drawing room or around the tea-table, was all politely on the surface. It was often made up of clichéd conver-sational gambits, as when Jack starts to speak to Gwendolen in Act I by mentioning the weather, a subject which is a cliché of English conversation because it is the height of good manners; the weather cannot, after all, be construed as controversial:

JACK: Charming day it has been, Miss Fairfax.

GWENDOLEN: Pray don't talk to me about the weather, Mr Worthing. Whenever people talk to me about the weather, I always feel quite certain that they mean something else. And that makes me so nervous. (Act I, p. 263)

This tiny exchange exemplifies the style of much of the play. An innocent remark about the weather, a perfectly proper and wholly artificial remark (does anyone really want to talk about 'charming' weather?), is shown to be a mere conventional surface. What Gwendolen's response points out here is that language is at its most deceptive when it is also at its most respectable. Jack's remark is what a linguist would term a **phatic** remark: that is, it serves no real function, expresses no real information, but acts only as a way of getting a conversation started. What Jack actually wants to talk about is his love for Gwendolen. But he has to take a circuitous route to get to talk about the real matter in hand. This is a world in which calling a spade a spade, as Cecily later suggests, is socially improper. Language here is **periphrastic** (the noun is **periphrasis**) – it speaks around a subject rather than addressing its subject directly. The characters in the play are very articulate and fluent. The speeches should not be rushed, but should be spoken slowly and extremely clearly, perhaps even with an exaggerated diction, and the accents are clearly upper-class (even for the servants who ape their masters' manners very successfully).

Oscar Wilde was very interested throughout his writing career in artifice. His characters are unnaturally eloquent. They rarely break up their speeches with the hesitations of real speech (the 'ums' and 'ers' that most people utter in everyday life). This exaggerated fluency of language is therefore one of the markers the play's anti-**naturalist** stance. The inconsequentiality of the language is related to the inconsequentiality of the plot discussed above. If the plot does not matter much, what better way to dramatise its unimportance than in a language which refuses to be simply expressive.

There are exceptions, of course. Strong emotion sometimes breaks through the veneer of polite conversation. When Jack declares his love for Gwendolen, for example, he is so nervous that all his conversational polish deserts him: 'Miss Fairfax, ever since I met you I have admired you more than any girl … I have ever met since … I met you', is what he manages to force out (Act I, p. 263), which is scarcely coherently put. Something similar happens to Algy when he is required by Cecily to dictate his passion to her so that she can put it into her diary for future reference:

ALGERNON: … Ahem! Ahem!

CECILY: Oh, don't cough, Ernest. When one is dictating one should speak fluently and not cough. Besides, I don't know how to spell a cough. [Writes as Algernon speaks.]

ALGERNON: [*speaking very rapidly*] Cecily, ever since I first looked upon your wonderful and incomparable beauty, I have dared to love you wildly, passionately, devotedly, hopelessly.

CHECK THE FILM
Anthony Asquith's film version of the play makes this point very effectively. The language is spoken with the exaggerated slowness and clarity of diction that was common on the stage for most of the first part of the twentieth century. This is not, as William Wordsworth might have put it, the language really spoken by men.

CECILY: I don't think that you should tell me that you love me wildly, passionately, devotedly, hopelessly. Hopelessly doesn't seem to make much sense, does it? (Act II, p. 286)

CHECK THE NET

The website developed to market Brian Gilbert's 1998 biopic *Wilde*, contains some very useful contextual material. As well as the expected interviews with cast and crew, there are also articles by the screenwriter and director who discuss Wilde's life with knowledge and sympathy. Go to **http://www. oscarwilde.com/** to access this resource.

The cough, followed by the speed of Algy's declaration of love, which stand in contrast to the more normally modulated and fluent tones of the play, suggest that Algy has lost control of himself in this short episode, an unusual position for him to find himself in. Add to that his loss of **semantic** control (the control of the meanings of the words he utters, as when he calls his love 'hopeless' despite Cecily engagement to him) and one can see a character under severe (though nonetheless comic) stress. And both Miss Prism and Canon Chasuble suffer similar linguistic flutterings when in each other's presence.

The character most in control of her language, just as, at the outset, she is most in control of the situation, is Lady Bracknell, who is formidably articulate, speaking a language which steam-rollers other members of the cast into submission. Lady Bracknell never surrenders this linguistic control partly because she is never in love; even when the rest of the plot goes against her in its **dénouement** of Jack's engagement to Gwendolen, her speech remains stable. The reader/spectator should think about the length of her speeches. Because this is a conversational play in which most of the action takes place in speech, speeches tend to be quite short with rapid exchanges between speakers. If **repartee** is a term from fencing in which small verbal gestures are exchanged to score points off the opponent, then Lady Bracknell, with her crescendos of comic indignation, is clearly carrying much heavier weaponry. It is powerful weaponry too, because it is so skilfully wielded that Lady Bracknell tempts her interlocutors into a loss of manners and temper; the play charts a social game, and those who behave rudely or lose control are the losers. The older woman knows this game extremely well, enjoys using language as a social weapon and takes pleasure in tempting Jack, for example, to forget his manners when she taunts him with a passing remark:

Mr Worthing, is Miss Cardew at all connected with any of the larger railway stations in London? I merely desire information. Until yesterday I had no idea that there were any families or persons whose origin was a Terminus. [JACK *looks perfectly furious, but restrains himself.*] (Act III, p. 303)

In the play as a whole, then, those who are most powerful in linguistic terms are also most socially powerful. Gwendolen, who shares her mother's linguistic prowess, will inherit her mantle. Jack, whose language is least secure, will be acted on by circumstance, rather than acting in his own behalf. For Oscar Wilde in *The Importance of Being Earnest*, language is character.

STAGING

The Importance of Being Earnest was first staged at the St James Theatre, London, on 14 February 1895. Like almost all contemporary theatres, the St. James had a **proscenium arch** stage. That is, the stage space was almost entirely behind a framed facade, so that if a room were depicted on the stage, as in *Earnest's* Acts I and II, three of the walls were behind the facade, and the audience made up an imaginary fourth wall.

This was the stage which had developed for the playing of **naturalistic** drama, in which the audience was supposed to suspend its disbelief, and to enter into a pretence that what was enacted before them was real. In naturalistic drama, the imaginary fourth wall was impenetrable. Actors on the stage never disrupted the illusion of reality in which they participated by, for example, addressing the audience directly. The action took place as if no audience were present. The period in which *Earnest* was first performed was one in which naturalism was the dominant mode. Stage sets were elaborately realistic, with real furniture, and massive attention to detail. Costumes for contemporary drama were often ordered from London and Paris couturiers. Everything was set up to heighten the illusion of reality. The original staging of Oscar Wilde's play drew heavily on this tradition. The anonymous reviewer for *The Stage* of 21 February 1895 drew attention to just one of the effects:

> Many were struck with the realistic watering-pot carried by Miss Evelyn Millard [playing Cecily] in the Second Act. From the

? QUESTION
Discuss the advantages and disadvantages of a naturalistic staging of *The Importance of Being Earnest*. You may choose alternatively to discuss the advantages and disadvantages of a staging which emphasizes artifice.

rose of this what looked like real water was distributed over the mimic garden. The water was merely silver sand. (Quoted in Jonathan Goodman, *The Oscar Wilde File*, 1988, pp. 31–2)

This is an interesting detail because, at first sight, it seems so unnecessary. Why not use real water? The answer is probably that the rose garden at Jack's country estate was made using silk flowers which would not have taken well to being really wet. An elaborate illusion was constructed to make artifice look like nature. The costumes and the sets were also made to look as real as possible. The original audiences, made up largely of middle- and upper-class theatre-goers, were looking at houses and gardens which closely resembled the ones they actually lived in – or houses and gardens in which they would have liked to live. The clothes on the stage were their clothes. The on-stage characters, therefore, were in some sense themselves. When they laughed at the ridiculous contortions of language and behaviour on the stage, they were also to some extent mocking their own morals and manners.

After Oscar Wilde's disgrace shortly after the opening of the play, all his West End runs were curtailed. *The Importance of Being Earnest* was the first of the plays to be rehabilitated, with several performances before the Great War. As time went on, however, it became increasingly clear that the play is quite specifically dated. The last professional 'modern-dress' performance, with the play set in contemporary London, was in 1923. Whilst the jokes in the play remain funny and fresh, the setting demands a world in which the trains run very frequently and on time, in which no-one has a car or a telephone, in which the upper classes routinely have large numbers of servants, where men wear detachable shirt cuffs, and in which women are closely chaperoned. Even in 1923, these things were no longer true. Since the 1920s then, the play has always therefore been staged as a period piece, set in a relatively innocent past, and apparently distanced from more modern concerns. Where the original audience saw itself – in modified but recognisable form – more recent audiences tend to view the play with nostalgia, and to see the satire as directed at a long-gone age.This does not mean, of course, that experimental staging is not possible. If *Earnest* always looked and sounded the same, it would not remain a popular play.

CHECK THE BOOK

John Stokes in *Oscar Wilde: Myths, Miracles and Imitations* discusses a number of recent productions of Wilde's plays in the West End. Notable amongst these is the 1993 production, directed by Nicholas Hytner, at the Aldwych Theatre. Part of the 'experimentalism' of this performance was its attempt to bring to the surface the play's gay subtext. On their first meeting in Act I, Algy (played by Richard E. Grant) and Jack (Alex Jennings) greeted each other with a kiss.

There have been notable experiments with **drag** casts, for example:
Lady Bracknell and Miss Prism seem perfect figures to be played by
men in women's clothing, and this kind of experiment accords well
with the play's **camp** attitudes. Moreover, most British theatres built
since the Second World War have **apron stages**, which jut out into the
audience. Instead of the audience all sitting in front of the action as
with a cinema screen, making up a 'fourth wall' to the action, the
apron stage has the audience sitting on three sides of the action, with a
backdrop making the fourth wall. *Earnest* has also been played **'in the
round'**, where the stage is entirely surrounded by the audience. These
alternative stagings have interesting effects on the relationship
between the cast and the audience. Where in the **proscenium arch**
theatre, the audience plays no part in the action since all attention is
focused on the stage, in apron and in-the-round productions,
members of the audience can see other members of the audience
across the stage. Moreover, the cast and the audience are much closer
to each other – there is no orchestra pit separating them. In more
modern stagings, the illusion is laid bare. We are not asked to suspend
our disbelief, to enter the illusory world of the stage; rather we are
required to notice that it is an illusion. This is one of the places in
which to seek a distinction between a **naturalist** and a **modernist**
response to the play: is the illusion convincing, as in naturalist drama,
or does the production draw attention to itself, as in a modernist
response? Since the play is largely about the complexity of the
relationships between nature and artifice, reality and illusion, reality
and appearance, modern stage formations help to point this message
out when they explicitly involve the audience's responses.

I've suggested already that the language of the play is artificial and
stylised. The same kinds of things might be said about its gestures
and choreography. If the speeches have to spoken in a measured
way, then perhaps movement should also be measured. Here, period
costume helps. The clothes worn by women in particular in the
1890s were highly elaborate. Long skirts, leg o' mutton sleeves and
corsetry all have their effect on the ways in which one is able to
move. An actress (or actor) in a corset has to stand up very straight,
and has also to think about her breathing since a corset presses on
the diaphragm, making spontaneity almost hazardous. Formal
clothes lead to formal speech and gesture. The play certainly cannot
be staged with characters in informal costumes.

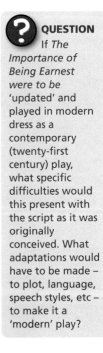

QUESTION
If *The
Importance of
Being Earnest*
were to be
'updated' and
played in modern
dress as a
contemporary
(twenty-first
century) play,
what specific
difficulties would
this present with
the script as it was
originally
conceived. What
adaptations would
have to be made –
to plot, language,
speech styles, etc –
to make it a
'modern' play?

? QUESTION
Write an essay in which, using your knowledge of *The Importance of Being Earnest*, you 'cast' it for a fantasy production of your own. You should name actors and actresses for each of the parts, and briefly describe your reasons for your casting choices.

It is an explicit part of Algy's character that he is a dandy with an exaggerated interest in his own appearance. Gwendolen is very 'smart' (Act I, p. 261). Compared to these two urban sophisticates, Jack and Cecily are supposed to look dowdy, but their plain dress is only plain relative to the splendour of their prospective spouses. Miss Prism may be sartorially challenged; but Lady Bracknell is most emphatically well-dressed. Costume provides the audience with visual clues to the meaning of character.

On the modern stage, sets for *Earnest* are seldom naturalistic. Very few props are needed to signal a room or a garden; light can be used to make distinctions between inside and outside locations. And if there is less to see on the stage, there is more emphasis on the cast. In modern minimal settings, the sense that the actors are playing characters who are themselves play-acting comes across very strongly, throwing up once again the issue of the illusory nature of the theatrical experience for the audience's consideration.

PART FOUR

CRITICAL HISTORY

RECEPTION AND EARLY CRITICAL VIEWS

The earliest reviewers of *The Importance of Being Earnest* were almost unanimous in their praise of the play, its performance and its writing. The critics emphasised above all else that the play had made its audience laugh. A number of reviewers noted a resemblance between Oscar Wilde's wit and that of W.S. Gilbert, the librettist of Gilbert and Sullivan fame, but also a playwright in his own right. Some also noted that plot devices in the play were derived from French farces. And the reviewer for the *New York Times* noted its resemblance to *Charley's Aunt* (1892), Brandon Thomas's farce which had the distinction of being the most popular and longest running play on the West End stage of the 1890s. Almost all agreed, nonetheless, that it was an impressively original play, with such an array of humour that there was something in it for everyone.

There was a little dissension within individual reviews, possibly because so many people disliked Oscar Wilde the man. William Archer found it a difficult play to write about because it had no substance, raised no moral point and so gave nothing for the critic to discuss. Similarly, an unsigned review in the magazine *Truth* for 21 February 1895 began: 'I have not the slightest intention of criticising Mr. O. Wilde's new piece at the St. James's: as well might one sit down after dinner and attempt gravely to discuss a *soufflé*.' Its virtues were entirely bound up with its humour.

Of the critics, only George Bernard Shaw disliked it. Given that Shaw regarded the theatre as a serious venue for political action, this is hardly a surprise. Although he found *Earnest* funny, he commented that he preferred 'to be moved to laughter, not to be tickled or bustled into it'. Shaw's own plays are very far removed from Oscar Wilde's, and the fact that Oscar Wilde had such a large and happy West End audience probably did not improve his temper.

 CHECK THE BOOK

Karl Beckson, ed., *Oscar Wilde: The Critical Heritage* (1971) reprints Wilde's original reviews with helpful critical apparatus. Jonathan Goodman's *The Oscar Wilde File* (1988) is a very useful supplement to Beckson's text.

CRITICAL HISTORY

The subsequent critical history of the play is entirely bound up with Oscar Wilde's own reputation. Only a few weeks after it opened, he was involved in the scandal that eventually led to his imprisonment. *Earnest*, given the positive reviews, could probably have expected an extended run in the St James, followed by a popular tour in the provinces. Oscar Wilde's disgrace put an immediate halt to that. *An Ideal Husband*, which had been playing to packed houses since January, came off the day after Oscar Wilde's arrest. *The Importance of Being Earnest* continued to play in the St James for a few weeks, though Oscar Wilde's name had been removed from the advertising hoardings and playbills. It could not, however, sustain its audience in the face of Oscar Wilde's imprisonment. Thereafter, for two generations, Oscar Wilde's name was mud, and to be interested in his works was seen as a very suspect preference. Despite the hostility to Oscar Wilde the man, there were professional revivals of *The Importance of Being Earnest* as early as 1902, produced by George Alexander, the original director; Alexander brought *Earnest* back to the West End no fewer than four times between Oscar Wilde's death in 1900 and the outbreak of the Great War in 1914. Alexander did not, however, return Oscar Wilde's name to the advertising hoardings until 1909. It is to be assumed that this play could be rehabilitated for a public hostile to Oscar Wilde's reputation because it apparently has so little reference to reality.

While the play has remained commercially successful, Oscar Wilde's reputation has taken a long time to recover. In the 1920s, for example, the novelist Arnold Bennett confidently asserted that Oscar Wilde was never a 'first-rate' writer, and that even *The Importance of Being Earnest* lacked 'the elements of permanence'. In the forties, Graham Hough's *The Last Romantics* regards Oscar Wilde as a mere poseur with nothing authentic or interesting to say. These are both judgements at least as much of the man as of his work, with a distaste for Oscar Wilde's sexual preferences attaching itself to the aesthetic judgements of the critics. They were not universal views, though. French and German critics very quickly came to Oscar Wilde's rescue in their own countries and their own languages. He has been highly regarded in Europe more or less since his disgrace.

CHECK THE FILM

Brian Gilbert's 1998 film *Wilde*, starring Stephen Fry as Wilde is the last in this line of positive portrayals of the playwright.

The view in Britain has taken longer to modify, and the process can perhaps be charted from the publication in 1957 of the Wolfenden Report, which recommended the repeal of the statute under which Oscar Wilde was convicted, and the actual repeal in 1967. There were two relatively sympathetic films about Oscar Wilde's life in the early 1960s. And since around 1970, there has been a plethora of books and articles which see Oscar Wilde in a positive light.

The Importance of Being Earnest and its author are now so respectable that the play has been accepted since 1993 as a suitable text for fourteen-year-old school-children to read as part of the United Kingdom's National Curriculum. Oscar Wilde's trials and conviction have also skewed the reception of the play in another direction. In 1895, Oscar Wilde was forty-one – a relatively young man. He cannot have believed that *The Importance of Being Earnest* would be his last West End production. But the play is now often read as though it is the conscious climax of his career, when Oscar Wilde himself described it as a play 'written by a butterfly for butterflies' and did not regard it as his best work. He might well have been rather displeased that *Earnest* is the text on which his reputation rests. However pleasurable we may find it, it is only accidentally Oscar Wilde's last word.

CONTEMPORARY APPROACHES

STRUCTURALIST READINGS

Structuralist readings of literature derive from the writings of the Swiss linguist, Ferdinand de Saussure. Saussure argued that language is not naturally related to the reality it attempts to describe. He elucidated three basic rules from which structuralist thought is derived.

 CHECK THE BOOK
For a really helpful and approachable account of the basics of structuralist theory, see Peter Barry, *Beginning Theory*.

- Words and things are related only arbitrarily

- Words have their meanings only by conventional agreement

- Meaning is consequently dependent on difference: we understand the concept 'hat' because it differs in sound or meaning from the words 'fat' or 'hit'. The words do not have intrinsic meanings, but have meanings which depend on their relation to other words

These ideas became significant for the reading of literary texts when they were taken up by French writers such as Claude Lévi-Strauss and Roland Barthes in the middle years of the twentieth century. Lévi-Strauss and Barthes both argued that all ways of signifying meaning between people could be similarly reduced to rules of arbitrariness, convention and difference. The food we eat, the clothes we wear as well as the way we talk to each other are all signifying systems, which convey messages to other people, but which do so in arbitrary and conventional ways.

This kind of insight can be useful for looking at all kinds of drama in performance. As well as the words that characters speak, settings, lighting and costumes are all part of the **semiotic** experience – 'semiotic' refers to all the different sign systems which generate the meaning of the performance. In *The Importance of Being Earnest*, how characters are dressed, for example, tells you something about them before they ever open their mouths. When Jack enters in mourning clothes in Act II, for example, he is wearing a costume which conventionally signals grief. The fact that Jack is actually mourning the death of a non-existent relative, his wicked brother Ernest, demonstrates the extent to which a sign (mourning clothes) may have no actual relationship with lived reality (Jack is not actually mourning anyone).

CHECK THE BOOK

To follow up on a quasi-structuralist reading of the play, see Jonathan Dollimore, *Sexual Dissidence: Augustine to Wilde, Freud to Foucault* (1991); Norbert Kohl's *Oscar Wilde: The Works of a Conformist Rebel* (1989) also offers some insights along these lines.

This play, however, also plays extensively with the fact that spoken and written language are only arbitrarily connected to reality. Think, for example, about the number of lies in the play: Jack lies about Ernest and about his ward 'little Cecily' who he terms his aunt; Algy about Bunbury, about cucumber sandwiches and about being Ernest; Cecily and Gwendolen both write patently fabricated diaries which masquerade as the facts of their lives; and even Lady Bracknell admits to a lie when she tells the assembled company that she has allowed Lord Bracknell to believe that Gwendolen is at a university lecture to explain her absence from home. This is a play where language has largely lost its functions of informing people about what is going on or of producing action, as when direct commands are ignored in the play. Words are useless here. They operate merely to keep social life going. Even Canon Chasuble, whose words, because he is a clergyman, are supposed to articulate a divine truth, speaks uselessly and his sermons have no effect.

A structuralist critic pays close attention to the structures of language. One of the structures with which *The Importance of Being Earnest* is concerned is that of the **binary opposition**. A binary opposition is a two-term structure in which opposing ideas exist on either side of an imaginary dividing line. Structuralist critics argue that such oppositions organise our thinking system. Examples from the play include: triviality versus seriousness (or triviality versus importance); lies versus truth; surface versus depth; young versus old; female versus male; city versus country; artifice versus nature. In each case from the above list, the first of the two terms of the opposition has traditionally be seen as less valuable than the second – lies are worse than truth, or again, to be natural is better than to be artificial. The play, however, overturns the traditional values of these oppositions, and in doing so, it points out both that the oppositions themselves are arbitrary, but also that the behaviour they demand is also arbitrary. A function in language, like binary opposition, extends its relevance in Oscar Wilde's play to issues of proper behaviour and morality.

HISTORICIST READINGS

An **historicist** approach to any literary text suggests that the text must be understood in relation to an historical perspective. As historicist critics, we must consider carefully both the original conception and reception of the text; but we must also remember that we also live in an historical period, and that therefore our responses to and preoccupations with the text are partly determined by our own time in history.

Historicist approaches are particularly appropriate when thinking about dramatic texts, since a play has two different kinds of history which interact with each other. It is a written script, with a publication history and history of critical reception in literary terms. But it also has a history of different performances which have taken place over time. In the case of *The Importance of Being Earnest*, a frequently revived play, it is a fascinating study for the critic to consider how, in the century since it was first performed, productions of the play have altered. The historicist critic might approach the play's performance history to place the play in its own right, but also to think about what subsequent performances can tell

CHECK THE BOOK

For examples of historicist readings see: Regenia Gagnier, *Idylls of the Marketplace: Oscar Wilde and the Victorian Public* (1986); Kerry Powell, *Oscar Wilde and the Theatre of the 1890s* (1990); Peter Raby, ed., *The Cambridge Companion to Oscar Wilde* (1997, especially the essays by Richard Allen Cave, Joel Kaplan and Kerry Powell); and John Stokes, *Oscar Wilde: Myths, Miracles and Imitations* (1996).

us about the age in which the performance took place. Equally, the critic might consider and try to reconstruct as far as possible, the original performance of the play. Is the play typical of its period or does it move away from the conventions of its own era? How did the original production look? How was it lit? How did its audiences respond? These are questions that an historicist critic might attempt to answer.

QUEER THEORY AND GAY CRITICISM

For over a century now, Oscar Wilde has been the anglophone world's most famous homosexual writer. This has meant that gay critics and critics interested in alternative sexualities have found him a very fruitful source for criticism. There has been a marked tendency to connect the life to the work, as if the fact of Oscar Wilde's sexual activities were somehow an adequate explanation for his work.

Since Susan Sontag used *The Importance of Being Earnest* as her keynote text in defining the mode of **camp** in her essay 'Notes on Camp', the play has often been read as a gay play. Sontag identified camp as an attitude to the world which was ironic, stylised and artificial and which engages in the reversal of the usual values of **binary oppositions**. Sontag does not say that camp is necessarily a homosexual mode, but her essay strongly implies a relationship between camp and gay sensibilities. Following from her lead, several critics have suggested a homoerotic subtext for the play. They point especially to Jack and Algy's relationship; they read Bunburying as a code word for illicit sexual activity; and they point to a possible pun on the words Earnest/*uraniste*, because *uraniste* was a contemporary word for a homosexual man. They also point out that it emerged at Oscar Wilde's trials that he habitually gave his same-sex partners engraved cigarette cases as gifts, which suggests a secret meaning to Jack's outraged exclamation to Algy in Act I: 'It is a very ungentlemanly thing to read a private cigarette case' (p. 256).

Gay criticism of *Earnest*, then, until very recently, has assumed that the play is indeed a gay play. The focus has been on the hidden meanings of the play which are available only to those 'in the know'. The critics have discussed the extent to which Oscar Wilde's play disguises its illicit content, so that the play manages to be

? QUESTION
To what extent is it possible and/or desirable to stage *The Importance of Being Earnest* as exemplifying a gay sensibility?

acceptable both to conservative audiences who do not see the hidden content, and to radical audiences who do. The two types of audience laugh at different things.

More recently, gay criticism has moved away from an easy identification of the play with the author's homosexuality. The plot of the play, after all, celebrates heterosexual marriage. Moreover, if a gay content is easily discernible, the play could never have been staged in the violently **homophobic** 1890s. Writers such as Alan Sinfield, Neil Bartlett and Joseph Bristow argue instead that it is not so much that the play itself is a gay play; rather, it is that Oscar Wilde has come to signify 'gayness' to contemporary society. The identification of the play as gay is a phenomenon that depends on the concerns of its audiences rather than on the intrinsic values the play itself espouses.

CHECK THE BOOK
For further information see: Neil Bartlett, *Who Was that Man? A Present for Mr. Oscar Wilde* (1989); Patricia Flannegan Behrendt, *Oscar Wilde: Eros and Aesthetics* (1991); Joseph Bristow, *Effeminate England: Homoerotic Writing after 1885* (1995); Alan Sinfield, *The Wilde Century: Effeminacy, Oscar Wilde and the Queer Moment* (1994); and Susan Sontag, 'Notes on Camp' in *A Susan Sontag Reader* (1983), pp. 105–20.

PART FIVE

BACKGROUND

OSCAR WILDE'S LIFE AND WORKS

The events of Oscar Wilde's life are relatively well-known. His is a story that has been popular with biographers because it has the shape of a Greek tragedy: a rapid rise to fame, followed by swift and sudden disgrace and ruin. This narrative shape makes a good tale. Whilst only one of his works (his prison letter *De Profundis*, 1905) is directly autobiographical and there is seldom any simple connection between his life and his writing, responses to Oscar Wilde's works have been directly related to responses to the story of his life. Oscar Wilde himself said to the French novelist André Gide: 'Do you want to know the great drama of my life? It's that I have put my genius into my life; all I've put into my works is my talent.' With the exception of *The Importance of Being Earnest* and occasionally of Oscar Wilde's only novel, *The Picture of Dorian Gray* (1891), critics have tended to agree with that judgement. Oscar Wilde was a deliberate self-publicist. He saw his personality as an intrinsic part of his work, and posterity has colluded with Oscar Wilde's own judgement. So whilst no writer's life directly 'explains' his/her work, in the case of Oscar Wilde, some sense of his biographical context is indispensable to the student of his writings.

CHECK THE BOOK

Wilde's best – and most comprehensive – biographer is Richard Ellmann in *Oscar Wilde* (1987). Many other versions of his life exist, some of which are marred by inconsistency and inaccuracy. Those interested in psycho-biographical approaches to his life could consider Melissa Knox's *Oscar Wilde: A Long and Lovely Suicide* as a supplement to Ellmann's magisterial tome.

Oscar Fingal O'Flahertie Wills Wilde (he quipped that this was not so much a name as a sentence) was born in Dublin in 1854 to an upper-middle-class Protestant family. He was the second son of Sir William Wilde, an eminent eye surgeon, and of Jane Wilde, usually known as Francesca, who wrote Irish Nationalist poetry under the name of Speranza (Italian for hope).

The Wilde family were at the centre of Dublin's intellectual life in the 1850s and 1860s, with Lady Wilde hosting regular soirées for poets, writers and politicians. Both of Oscar Wilde's parents were interested in Irish politics, and both were involved in recovering native Irish culture, in particular the folk-tales and fairy stories of the Irish peasantry. They were comfortably off, but they also provided their children (Oscar and his elder brother Willie) with a rich cultural background.

Oscar was educated first at the Portora Royal School in Enniskillen, and then at Trinity College, Dublin, where he achieved a first in Classics. Following this academic triumph, he was awarded a scholarship to Magdalen College, Oxford, to study Literae Humaniores (Greek and Roman philosophy and literature, also sometimes known as the 'Greats' syllabus), which he took up in 1874. From then on, he spent the majority of his life in England, and he regarded coming to England as one of the turning points of his life.

At Oxford, Oscar Wilde proved again to be a brilliant scholar, though he was also often in trouble with the college authorities for small acts of disobedience. Nonetheless, he achieved a double first in his degree course, and when he left Oxford in 1878, he had also won the Newdigate prize for poetry for his poem 'Ravenna'. He hoped that all the world would soon be at his feet, though it actually took him a considerable time to become established as a writer and critic.

From Oxford he went to London, where he lived off the rents of some of the Irish property that his father had left him (Sir William had died in 1876); and he set about becoming famous in the capital. In 1881, he published his first volume of *Poems*, works which are not much read today, and which were not especially well received at the time; reviewers felt that they were derivative. All the same, *Poems* had one important effect. They brought to Oscar Wilde an invitation to go on a lecture tour to the United States in 1882, which he did, declaring to American customs officers on his arrival that he had nothing to declare but his genius. The lecture-tour came about at the instigation of the opera impresario, Richard D'Oyly Carte, who promoted the works of Gilbert and Sullivan. In 1881, Gilbert and Sullivan had produced a satiric operetta entitled *Patience; or, Bunthorne's Bride*, which mocked the pretensions of the Aesthetic Movement in England. The aesthetes, under the influence of the Pre-Raphaelite poets and painters, of the critic Walter Pater, and of the Arts and Crafts Movement of William Morris, professed that art and beauty were the most important values in a society. D'Oyly Carte was worried that Americans would not understand the satire in *Patience* because they had no aesthetic movement of their own. He therefore commissioned Oscar Wilde to lecture on 'The English Aesthetic Movement', 'The House Beautiful' and 'Aesthetic Dress' as

 CHECK THE NET
A short version of Wilde's biography, along with a chronology of the major events of his life and the dates of his writings can be found on the Victorian Web site. Go to **http://www. victorianweb.org** to access this information.

part of the promotion of the opera. The Gilbert and Sullivan connection is significant in *The Importance of Being Earnest* for two reasons. Firstly, when Jack and Algy re-enter the scene at the beginning of Act III, they are whistling 'some dreadful popular air from a British Opera' (Act III, p. 300) which may very well be a reference to Sir Arthur Sullivan's music. Secondly, the reviewers of the play commented, almost to a man, that *Earnest* contained elements of Gilbertian farce (see Reception and Early Critical Views).

CHECK THE BOOK

Gary Schmidgall's *The Stranger Wilde: Interpreting Oscar* (1994) contains a very full account of Wilde's American tour.

Oscar Wilde's career proper, then, began in advertising. Ostensibly he was advertising Gilbert and Sullivan, but he was also advertising himself. The tour was quite a success, and it helped to make Oscar Wilde's name, in particular because of his flamboyant style of dress, and his exaggerated lecturing style; his intonation, pronunciation and inflexions as he spoke his lectures caused much comment at the time.

According to Richard Ellmann, the American papers were fascinated by his clothes when his ship docked in January 1882: they described him at length as wearing 'a great green coat that hung down almost to his feet ... the collar and cuffs were trimmed with seal or otter and so was the material for the round cap, variously described as a smoking cap or a turban. Beneath the coat could be discerned a shirt with a wide Lord Byron collar and a sky-blue necktie, vaguely reminiscent of the costume of a modern mariner. He wore patent leather shoes on his small feet.' (Richard Ellmann, *Oscar Wilde*, pp. 150–1) His hair was also long and curled. None of this sounds particularly outrageous to us. It is important to remember, however, that the Victorian gentleman's clothes were generally black or grey, and certainly did not call attention to themselves; and a gentleman's hair would be close-cropped. To wear clothes like the ones Oscar Wilde wore was the gesture of a flagrant self-publicist, a dandy figure. And many of the male characters Oscar Wilde would describe in his writing career, including Algy in *The Importance of Being Earnest*, would pay similar attention to their costumes.

CONTEXT

In 'Phrases and Philosophies for the Use of the Young', Wilde comments: 'The only way to atone for being occasionally a little over-dressed is by being always absolutely over-educated'.

On his return to England, Oscar Wilde toured the country, giving lectures about his impressions of America. At the same he was also courting a young lady named Constance Lloyd, the woman he was eventually to marry in 1884. Constance was the daughter of a well-to-do Irish lawyer, and their marriage was a love-match. They seem to have been very happy for the first two or three years of their time together, and they had two sons, Cyril (born in 1885) and Vyvyan (born in 1886).

With these new family responsibilities, along with the expenses of keeping up his brilliantly furnished and decorated family home in Tite Street, Chelsea (like Algy's rooms in *The Importance of Being Earnest*, Oscar Wilde's home was famous for being 'luxuriously and artistically furnished' – Act I, p. 253), it was imperative that Oscar Wilde should start to earn a proper and more assured living than lecture tours and occasional book reviewing could give him.

He therefore began to pursue a career in journalism, reviewing widely for the major magazines and, eventually, in 1887, he took up the editorship of a magazine entitled *The Lady's World*. His first act as editor was to change the magazine's name to *The Woman's World*. Under his editorship, the magazine published articles on dress reform (polemics against the corset), literary reviews and essays on subjects as diverse as votes for women and the modern theatre.

The magazine was a relative success, though Oscar Wilde soon became bored with the day-to-day routine of running it, and increasingly withdrew from the real work. He gave up the job in 1889.

During this period, Oscar Wilde made a point of knowing all the most famous and interesting people. He was a friend to the rich and famous, some of whom he got to write for his magazine. He was close to the actress Lily Langtry, mistress of the Prince of Wales, and to Sarah Bernhardt, the most famous actress of the day. He had a reputation as the most interesting and entertaining dinner guests, dazzling London society with his brilliant conversation. Lots of contemporary commentators, men like the Irish poet W.B. Yeats and the comic writer Max Beerbohm, marvelled at his fluency, exaggerated diction and his wit. He lived largely amongst the upper-middle-class and aristocratic milieu that he reproduced in *The Importance of Being Earnest*. It is the overblown polite, formal conversation of this social group that the play mimics and parodies. But for all his popularity and apparently stable family life, Oscar

CONTEXT

One of the rooms in Wilde's house was decorated by the American artist James Abott McNeill Whistler – just like Algy, his rooms were artistically furnished.

 CHECK THE BOOK

For an account of Wilde's period as editor of *The Woman's World*, see Laurel Brake's *Subjugated Knowledges* (1994).

Wilde had not yet actually written anything in the field of literature except for that slim volume of poems from 1881, published at his own expense, which languished largely unread even then.

From 1888 he began to remedy that omission. For the next seven years he was immensely productive. He began in 1888 with a volume of short stories for children, *The Happy Prince and Other Stories*, probably written with his own sons in mind, but also drawing on the legacy of his parents who had been so interested in Irish folk tales. This was followed up in 1891 by fairy stories for more adult readers, *A House of Pomegranates*. He published essays of theoretical criticism such as 'The Decay of Lying' and 'The Critic as Artist' which were eventually collected into a single volume called *Intentions* (1891). His short stories *Lord Arthur Saville's Crime and Other Stories* also came out in 1891. And his only novel, *The Picture of Dorian Gray*, was published in *Lippincott's Magazine* in 1890, and then as single-volume edition, also in 1891. His range is very wide. There are important essays such as 'The Soul of Man Under Socialism' (1891) alongside a poem called 'The Sphynx' (1894), a fantasia about the relationships between the ancient pagan world and Christian contemporary society. There was also an unperformed play, *Salomé*, written in French for Sarah Bernhardt in 1891, denied a licence for the English stage because it portrayed biblical characters, and eventually published in 1894 with illustrations by the artist Aubrey Beardsley.

CHECK THE BOOK

Jonathan Goodman's *The Oscar Wilde File* (1988) is a wonderful resource for students wishing to trace Wilde's successful theatrical career in the early 1890s. Goodman reprints reviews from the original performances of the plays as well as other contemporary material.

This prolific activity is not, however, what Oscar Wilde is now most famous for. He is best known as a playwright, who produced dazzling social comedies. From 1892–5, he almost dominated the West End stage with the plays which have made his reputation. He began with *Lady Windermere's Fan*, performed at the St James Theatre in 1892, and published a year later. This is a play about moral rectitude amongst the upper classes, and its message is that morality is not absolute. This was followed by *A Woman of No Importance* (performed in 1893, published in 1894). The play tells the story of a woman who has borne an illegitimate son and of her response (as well as the response of the son) to her seducer twenty years after the events that precipitated her disgrace. The wicked seducer, Lord Illingworth, has some of the best lines in the play, but he is defeated at the end. Next came *An Ideal Husband* (performed

1895, published 1899), a story of intrigue and blackmail that surrounds the ideal husband of the title, an upright politician with a secret misdemeanour in his past. These are all **realist** plays, though they also have their touches of the **melodramatic**. Unlike *Earnest*, they raise moral issues seriously, whilst also having comic structures (the good end happily and the bad less happily) and some very funny lines. Though none of them has ever been so popular as *The Importance of Being Earnest*, they all enjoy regular revivals. They were and are commercially successful plays.

When *The Importance of Being Earnest* was first staged in February 1895, it seemed that Oscar Wilde was at the height of his powers. *An Ideal Husband* was running in a neighbouring theatre, and his earlier two plays had been resounding successes. The world was at his feet, and it appeared that everything he touched was successful.

From around 1886, however, Oscar Wilde had been leading a double life. On the face of it in 1895, he was a happily married man, with two children whom he adored, and a wife with whom he got on. He had a successful career in literature and journalism. But at the same time, Oscar Wilde was also involved in a series of illicit homosexual affairs. This was an extremely dangerous activity at this period because, in 1885, the Criminal Law Amendment Act had criminalised all sexual activity between men, with a maximum sentence of two years imprisonment with hard labour for offenders.

In 1886, Oscar Wilde had met an Oxford undergraduate named Robert Ross, and had been seduced by him. From then on, Oscar Wilde increasingly sought sexual pleasure with young men, some from his own social milieu, but more often and more dangerously, with working-class rent-boys who supplemented their meagre incomes with casual prostitution, and often also with the casual blackmail of their clients. Oscar Wilde was certainly blackmailed, though mostly for relatively small sums, and he appears to have rather enjoyed the danger of these relationships.

Most dangerous of all, however, was his relationship with a young aristocrat named Lord Alfred Douglas, a son of the Marquess of Queensberry. Oscar Wilde first met Douglas around 1892 and became immediately and catastrophically infatuated with him,

CHECK THE BOOK

Ed Cohen's *A Talk on the Wilde Side* (1993) gives excellent background material on the 1885 Criminal Law Amendment Act and its implications. He also discusses in detail the Wilde trials and their aftermath.

CONTEXT

Queensberry – famous in his own lifetime for his establishment of the rules of modern boxing – led a very unsettled private life. He had been divorced twice, itself a scandal: from Douglas's mother for violence; from his second wife for non-consummation of their marriage. He was known as the 'Mad Marquess'.

despite Douglas's erratic character and uncertain temperament. (There were a number of quite violent confrontations between the two men.) The relationship had its own problems, and Oscar Wilde tried on several occasions to break off with Douglas, though he was always won back in the end. But the real problem arose when the Marquess of Queensberry became involved.

Queensberry was a very strange man with a peculiar sense of morality in his own private life.

Nonetheless, he believed that he had right on his side when he sought to break up the friendship between Oscar Wilde and his son. His methods were not subtle. He once arrived at Oscar Wilde's family home with two hired heavies to try to intimidate Oscar Wilde into giving Douglas up. When that failed, he went to the law.

Just as rehearsals for *The Importance of Being Earnest* were beginning at the St James in early 1895, Queensberry left an insulting message for Oscar Wilde at his club. The message, left on an open post-card read: 'To Oscar Wilde, posing as a somdomite' (Queensberry could not spell). When Oscar Wilde discovered the card a few weeks later, he decided, with Douglas's support, to sue the Marquess for criminal libel in April 1895; Queensberry entered a plea of justification and won the case. A warrant was issued for Oscar Wilde's arrest on the basis of the evidence of his homosexual relationships presented at the libel trial, and after two criminal trials, he was eventually found guilty of gross indecency and sentenced to two years imprisonment with hard labour. He served his sentence at Wandsworth and Reading. During his imprisonment, he was declared bankrupt to pay his legal costs, he lost the right to see his children, and though Constance never divorced him, she refused to have anything to do with him. His mother also died. Oscar Wilde was now a broken man. During his imprisonment, he wrote the letter now known as *De Profundis*, which is addressed to Douglas. Its aim is to explain his own actions, but also to make Douglas aware of his own responsibilities in Oscar Wilde's downfall. This letter was only published in full in 1962.

On his release in May 1897, Oscar Wilde went to France, and never returned to England. In France, he wrote the last of his published works, *The Ballad of Reading Gaol*, a reflection by a prisoner about a fellow inmate who had been condemned to death. The poem was published anonymously in 1898.

Following his imprisonment, Oscar Wilde was largely shunned by his former friends with a few honourable exceptions. The English abroad either insulted or ignored him. His wife changed her name to escape from the scandal he had brought on her, and he never saw her or his children again. He spent his last years in relative poverty, and was often lonely. He died in a Paris hotel in November 1900, joking that he was dying as he had lived, beyond his means, and that either he or the wallpaper had to go.

HISTORICAL BACKGROUND

On the face of it, Oscar Wilde's *The Importance of Being Earnest* might appear a timeless play, largely unrelated to the period in which it was written and first performed. It does not seem to have much to say about the official history of the 1890s, the parliamentary politics, the battles, the wars. There are one or two topical references, such as Jack's admission that he is a 'Liberal Unionist' (Act I, p. 267), or Lady Bracknell's question about whether the 'exploded' Bunbury was 'the victim of a revolutionary outrage' (Act III, p. 303), which refers to a number of anarchist bomb attacks that had taken place in the late 1880s and early 1890s. Apart from these, the play appears to have little to do with its context of production and performance. However, such a view holds true only if one takes a very narrow view of history. The play is, in fact, closely related to the social history, if not the political history, of the 1890s.

For example, one of the themes of the play is the relationship between the sexes – what are the respective roles of men and women? Although the theme is treated with humour, almost as though it does not matter at all, it was in fact a very topical issue for Oscar Wilde's contemporaries. The novelist George Gissing described the late nineteenth century as a period of 'sexual anarchy' because of the formal agitation by women for wider rights, in particular the rights to education, to enter the professions, and to

CHECK THE BOOK
For the full text of *De Profundis* with helpful notes, see Rupert Hart-Davis, *Selected Letters of Oscar Wilde* (1962). The letter is also reprinted in a Penguin edition as *Oscar Wilde, De Profundis and Selected Writings* and in Merlin Holland's *Complete Works of Oscar Wilde* (1994).

CHECK THE BOOK
Martha Vicinus's edited collection, *A Widening Sphere* (1977) contains a number of useful historical essays on the subject of the separate spheres debate.

vote. This was a matter for some anxiety because the traditional view of gender relations was that men were active, manly, assertive and economically independent, whilst women were assumed to be passive, feminine, pliant and dependent. From the middle of the nineteenth century, there had been numerous debates in newspapers and magazines about this view, with the conservative position of 'man for the field, woman for the hearth' largely holding sway.

The debate is known as the **separate spheres debate**, named after the assumption that a woman's proper sphere was in the home, a man's proper sphere in the public world of action and/or commerce. That it was a well-known debate can be charted by skimming through the pages of the satirical journal *Punch; or, The London Charivari* for the early nineties, where references to the problems of male/female relations abound.

Of course, not all women stayed at home in Victorian England. The majority of working-class women were workers outside the domestic sphere throughout Victoria's reign; by the end of the century, significant numbers of middle-class women were also seeking employment beyond the home. But these facts provoked severe reactions from old-fashioned men and women who saw the evidence of women in the labour market as a marker of social and moral decline. Male workers often felt threatened when women entered the workplace, often justifiably worried that women workers would depress wages because they were routinely paid less than men. And middle-class men feared a loss of status if their daughters (or, even more rarely, their wives) went out to work, since it implied that they could not be supported by the father's income alone. A man who could not properly support his family was not fulfilling his duties as a man.

CHECK THE BOOK
James Eli Adams' *Dandies and Desert Saints: Styles of Masculinity in Victorian England* (1994) describes the ideal concepts of masculinity in the Victorian period.

The Importance of Being Earnest makes extensive reference – both implicitly and explicitly – to this debate. The play as a whole, for example, shows the women characters to be far more powerful than the men. Jack's projected marriage to Gwendolen will be not be based on her dependence or pliability; she will be in charge of that relationship. Jack, as Lady Bracknell's questions of him demonstrate, is idle, effete and ineffectual. He has none of the traditional manly virtues of self-restraint, perseverance and self-reliance.

Algy's case is even more serious, for he shares all Jack's 'vices', but he is not even rich. Moreover, amongst the Bracknell women, this role reversal has been going on for at least a generation, with Lady Bracknell clearly ruling her own home, and her husband occupying a subordinate position. Gwendolen, speaking of her father to Cecily, says:

> My father is Lord Bracknell. You have never heard of papa, I suppose? … Outside the family circle, papa, I am glad to say, is entirely unknown. I think that is quite as it should be. The home seems to me to be the proper sphere for the man. And certainly, once a man begins to neglect his domestic duties, he becomes painfully effeminate, does he not? And I don't like that. It makes men so very attractive. (Act II, p. 290, my ellipsis)

The phrase 'the proper sphere', referring explicitly to the **separate spheres debate**, places this text in the 1890s. It was a very well-known concept for a late-nineteenth-century audience. But, of course, Gwendolen's views completely reverse the usual order in which the home is a woman's proper sphere, and in which a man who pays too much attention to his home life is regarded by contemporary society as effeminate. (This indeed was a criticism of Oscar Wilde himself, who had spent a small fortune on the interior decorations for his own Chelsea home.) For Oscar Wilde's original audiences, it is likely that the overturning of traditional gender roles was funny because it seemed so absurd and unlikely. Today's readers and viewers might have a different view.

With views like those Gwendolen expresses, the 1895 audience might well have defined her – and possibly Cecily too – as **New Women**. The term was coined in 1894 by the novelist Sarah Grand, to describe both women in literature and women in real life who were dissatisfied with their conventional roles and sought wider fields of action than mere domesticity. In positive descriptions of the New Woman, she was supposed to be intelligent, educated, active, employable and attractive. In negative versions, she was described as mannish, unwomanly, an immoral blue-stocking with no hope of ever marrying a decent man.

 CHECK THE BOOK

In recent years the figure of the New Woman has provoked a great deal of debate. See, for example, Ann Heilmann, *New Woman Fiction: Women Writing First-Wave Feminism* (2000), which reproduces some marvelous contemporary illustrations from the periodical press of the period; additionally, Sally Ledger's *The New Woman: Fiction and Feminism at the Fin de Siècle* (1997) and Lyn Pykett's *The Improper Feminine: The Woman's Sensation Novel and the New Woman Writing* (1992) all give significant information about this 1890's cultural phenomenon.

CONTEXT

That this was a typical matter for debate amongst 'advanced' women in the period is signalled by the fact that in E. M. Forster's 1910 novel, *Howards End*, the Schlegel sisters participate in a debating forum that considers precisely this question.

Gwendolen certainly has some of the features associated with the New Woman. She is a powerful figure, attractive and rich, and she apparently has intellectual pretensions. Her mother excuses Gwendolen's absence to Lord Bracknell by telling him that she has gone to a lecture 'by the University Extension Scheme on the Influence of a permanent income of Thought' (Act III, p. 302).

In the Bracknell household, this is clearly a suitable reason to be absent from home without a chaperone. Her views and her attitudes are ones which might well be associated with a new kind of emancipated woman.

Cecily's definition as a New Woman is perhaps less obvious. She certainly does not have intellectual ambitions, and spends a considerable part of the play avoiding lessons. She does, however, have a 'capital appetite' and goes for long walks (Act I, p. 271), suggesting that she is physically vigorous rather than conventionally and femininely enfeebled.

Oscar Wilde's play does not make it at all clear whether his audience is supposed to approve of assertive women or not. Clearly Lady Bracknell is terrifyingly unattractive. But Gwendolen and Cecily cloud the issue.

The correlative of the assertive woman in the play is the weak man. None of the men in the play could be described as ideal. If Jack and Algy are too lazy to be 'real' men, then Canon Chasuble and the absent Lord Bracknell represent the end result of attenuated masculine virtues: the Canon has no control over his world whatsoever; and Lord Bracknell is a character whose role in the world has been so diminished that he does not appear in the play at all, leaving the public face of his family to his wife and daughter. Even in his home, if there is an odd number for dinner, it is taken for granted that Lord Bracknell will dine upstairs and play no part in the social events which his wife arranges. In the world of the play, this ineffectuality is funny. But in the world beyond the play, there were real anxieties about gender reversal. Whilst the play appears on the one hand to be ahistorical and absurdist, it is, on the other, very closely placed in its own period, and is tapping a humour that depended on audience familiarity with its key ideas.

CONTEXT

In Bram Stoker's 1897 novel, *Dracula*, Mina Harker identifies herself as New Woman on the basis that she has a capital appetite and can cope with long vigorous country walks.

CHECK THE BOOK

For further information about the social, historical and political contexts of Oscar Wilde's play, see: Sally Ledger and Scott McCracken, eds, *Cultural Politics at the Fin de Siècle* (1995); Elaine Showalter, *Sexual Anarchy: Gender and Culture at the Fin de Siècle* (1990); and John Stokes, *In the Nineties*, (1989).

LITERARY BACKGROUND

GENERAL INFLUENCES

Oscar Wilde was not only a very well-educated man, with a fund of knowledge from his university studies; he was also very widely-read in contemporary literature and knew a lot about contemporary theatre, having worked as a reviewer for much of his career. It would be impossible therefore to enumerate all the influences on his writing. But there are some texts and writers whose influence on Oscar Wilde was long-lasting and very significant.

Amongst the important sources for Oscar Wilde's ideas is the critic and Oxford don, Walter Pater, whose book, *Studies in the History of the Renaissance* (1873), was described by Oscar Wilde as his 'golden book'. Oscar Wilde read *The Renaissance* during his first term at Oxford in 1874, soon after its publication, and he referred to Pater's ideas throughout his life. Pater was one of the founders of the aesthetic movement in art, literature and criticism. Most Victorian critics proceeded from the belief that literature and art were moral forces; a text was supposed accurately to reflect its own society, but it was also required to preach a moral lesson to the reader. Pater overturned this view, suggesting instead that all art forms are self-sufficient. The role of the critic is not to discern the text's morality; nor should he (Victorian criticism assumed male critics and readers) expend much effort in drawing connections between the real world and the text.

CHECK THE BOOK
Ruth Robbins' *Pater to Forster, 1873–1924* (2003) discusses Pater's ideas in some detail, and places them in the context of the nineteenth-century's critical establishment.

Rather the critic should pay careful attention to the craft or artistry of the piece in its own right. This required a particular kind of temperament in the critic, who had to be sensitive to his own impressions rather than to the more general effects of the text on the public at large. His criticism was therefore individualistic, impressionistic and divorced from moral imperatives. At the end of *The Renaissance*, Pater produced a manifesto for the artistic life. He suggested that one should live not for the consequences of one's actions, but rather for the moment, and the perfect moment was his ideal in both criticism and in life. His emphasis was on subjective feelings rather than on objective reality; it is certainly an anti-**realist** critical mode. Pater further argued that the critic's work was itself to be seen as a work of art. in *The Importance of Being Earnest*, this influence shows itself in almost every facet of the play. The inconsequential plot, the patterning of character, dialogue and action, all point to a non-realist world. This is a play without a **moral**. It exists for its own sake, for its own perfection. It communicates no message. As Algy says of his own epigram about women becoming like their mothers: 'It is perfectly phrased' (Act I, p. 270). Its perfect phrasing is all that matters; its truth value is utterly unimportant.

Earnest also draws on the traditions of the **comedy of manners**, as they were developed by the Restoration dramatists (Wycherley, Congreve, Etherege and Vanbrugh), as well as the eighteenth-century tradition of playwrights such as Richard Brinsley Sheridan and Oliver Goldsmith. From these traditions, Oscar Wilde took the fast-moving verbal exchanges, but in *Earnest*, he pared down the force of plots based on deception or cruelty, and turned these aspects into **farce**. In the traditional comedy of manners, unscrupulous characters get their way because of their superior intelligence. In Oscar Wilde's play, however, no-one is markedly intelligent; and the audience is deprived of the moral certainties of 'good' and 'bad'. Whilst we might prefer the young lovers to Lady Bracknell, she is not presented as a wicked woman. This is a matter of preference rather than an absolute moral position. We are not required to care about the characters or the outcome of the plot.

? QUESTION To what extent can *The Importance of Being Earnest* be understood as a social satire? Discuss with close reference to the play.

Oscar Wilde had certainly read widely in the fiction of his own time because he worked as a reviewer, and for the most part he disliked it. In the 1890s, the dominant mode in literary fiction was the **realist** novel. Realism is a disputed term, but for the late nineteenth century it broadly meant the attempt in fiction to portray ordinary life accurately. Plots would focus on so-called average people and the problems of their lives, in particular, love, romance, marriage, property and inheritance. In a society which still regarded marriage as the main building-block of social stability, and in which the discussion of sexual impropriety of any kind was forbidden in mixed company, there were vast swathes of subject matter that could not be touched upon. (The outraged reactions of contemporary readers to Thomas Hardy's *Tess of the D'Urbervilles* (1891) and *Jude the Obscure* (1895) demonstrated very clearly that the public who read the three-volume novel would not tolerate illegitimacy or extramarital sexuality as fit for representation.) This version of realism is clearly a very narrow definition of what constitutes reality; it might be helpful therefore to think of realism as a series of conventions by which a certain reality was supposed to be represented.

By the time Oscar Wilde was writing, he may have felt that the realist novel had become hidebound by its own conventions, suggested by the fact that we are supposed to laugh at Miss Prism's simplistic idea of a proper plot when she describes her own novel in Act II.

Oscar Wilde's essay 'The Decay of Lying' (published in *Intentions*, 1891) is not only an attack on realist and naturalist novelists such as George Meredith or Emile Zola; it also states explicitly that the imitation of reality is never the proper role of art. In *Earnest*, the patterns of language and action do not imitate lived reality. His play refuses the referentiality of realism (it does not refer to reality). The play is influenced by the writing of the period, but influenced in reaction against it, rather than in imitation of it.

IMMEDIATE INFLUENCES

There are two schools of thought about Oscar Wilde's response to the late-nineteenth-century professional stage. One argues that he left his own period behind him and that he is therefore a precursor of modernist and experimental drama. The other suggests that he was very much a writer of his own age. The truth probably lies somewhere between these two poles.

It is a commonplace of criticism of the Victorian theatre that very little of what Victorian audiences saw has survived, and this is often read (sometimes unjustifiably) as evidence of the poor quality of dramatic writing in the period. The real history of the Victorian theatre is still being uncovered, but it is already clear that there was a massive range of popular entertainments in London and the big British cities, from serious drama through to music-hall with its short-lived sketches and songs.

> **CONTEXT**
>
> Another mode of writing in Victorian fiction – one which was immensely popular from the 1860s onwards – was the so-called Sensation novel. Inaugurated by texts such as Wilkie Collins' *The Woman in White* (1860-1) and Mary Elizabeth Braddon's *Lady Audley's Secret* (1861-2), sensation novels focused on marital infidelity, intrigue, crime, deception and lunacy. When Gwendolen comments in Act II, that she always carries her diary with her – 'One should always have something sensational to read in the train' (Act II, p. 292) – she is making reference to precisely the kind of cheap fiction which Miss Prism has presumably tried to write.

CHECK THE BOOK
Kerry Powell, *Oscar Wilde and the Theatre of the 1890s* and Sos Eltis, *Revising Wilde* are both examples of texts which set out to uncover the lost history of the Victorian theatre. John Stokes' *In the Nineties* (1989) looks beyond the West End to the popular theatres and music halls of the period as well.

The kinds of theatre for which Oscar Wilde was writing were at the top end of the social spectrum. The West End catered for wealthy audiences, almost solely drawn from the middle and upper classes. This was an audience with its own sense of what was meant by respectability, and a strong belief that theatrical presentations had a moral imperative to reinforce the concept.

The serious plays this audience came to see in the 1890s largely belonged to a sub-genre called the problem play, a play which investigates a particular social problem. The most usual problem investigated by playwrights of the period was the so-called marriage problem. In an age when marriage was an ideal, when divorces remained extremely difficult to obtain, and when divorcees were the subjects of scandal and disgrace, British playwrights such as Henry Arthur Jones and Arthur Wing Pinero wrote numerous plays which investigated the plight of women driven to adultery by loveless marriages from which they could not legally escape, or of divorced women who had lost their social respectability on the dissolution of their marriages, and of women who had never married, having been seduced and abandoned by wicked upper-class debauchees.

By the time of Oscar Wilde's arrest and imprisonment, what was called the new drama was coming to prominence. This referred to drama with real intellectual content, plays which made its audiences think about social issues, rather than merely entertaining them. The plays of Henrik Ibsen such as *A Doll's House* (1879), or *Ghosts* (1881), considered seriously the issue of women's emancipation, or the social effects of syphilis. Writers like Ibsen examined more shocking issues more rigorously than home-grown writers like Pinero or Jones, though Ibsen's plays were known only to a small intellectual elite. And George Bernard Shaw was also starting to experiment with the genre of the problem play and the form of the well-made play (a play with a very closely structured plotting) in the 1890s, though his plays often had to wait for decades for performance because their subject matter was so shocking that they were denied licences for public performance by the Lord Chamberlain.

The Importance of Being Earnest clearly is not a problem play, but it does make reference to the genre. Lady Bracknell's discovery that

Jack is a foundling and his mis-identification of Miss Prism as his mother refer both to the problem play **motif** of female sexual activity, as well as to the **melodrama**.

Melodrama could, perhaps be described as a low cultural form. It was the theatre of the masses, of the urban working and lower-middle classes, who had to work hard for a living and wanted entertainment not intellectual stimulus from theatre, though its audiences were much more socially mixed than in the West End theatres where sheer expense kept the proletariat away.

The melodrama depended on creaking plots, filled with coincidence and sudden reversals of fortune. The characters were one-dimensional rather than psychologically convincing. It was exciting to look at, easy to follow and morally clear-cut. There were musical interludes, required by legislation: 'real' theatre had to seek licences from the Lord Chamberlain's office to put on serious plays for public performances, but musical plays were exempt. *Earnest* is not a melodrama either. There is music – but it is part of the action, used to establish character (as when Algy describes his playing as inaccurate though rendered with feeling, or when Jack and Algy pretend that they are unworried by the collapse of their love affairs by whistling the tune of 'some dreadful popular air from a British opera' – Act III, p. 300). Unlike melodrama, the scenes in *Earnest* are very long, and the audience has to concentrate to get the jokes. However, the plot is absurd, dependent on coincidence and reversal of fortune. The characters are not psychologically motivated and do not behave or speak realistically.

The genre of Oscar Wilde's play, one might say, is uncertain. This is important because it allows the playwright to signal clues from the various genres with which his audiences might be familiar, and then to upend their expectations. There are good jokes on the stage, but the audience is also laughing at its own recognitions and mis-recognitions of verbal, plot or character clues.

Oscar Wilde was very well versed in the theatrical codes of his day, to the extent that recent research has shown that his play borrows plot devices from other contemporary dramatists. Kerry Powell's book, *Oscar Wilde and the Theatre of the 1890s*, places Oscar Wilde

---

CONTEXT

In Wilde's novel *The Picture of Dorian Gray*, the young Dorian falls in love with an actress in an East End theatre – itself a plot from melodrama. Wilde's depiction of the theatre, with its noisy audience who joined in with Shakespeare's *Romeo and Juliet* as if it were a Christmas pantomime, perhaps gives some idea of what Wilde himself felt about melodramas and cheap theatre more generally.

CHECK THE BOOK

To get a flavour of Victorian melodrama conventions, see George Rowell ed., *Nineteenth-Century Plays* (1972), which reprints a number of infamous examples.

as a writer very much in tune with his time. He shows that the plot of *The Importance of Being Earnest* is partly derived from a play Oscar Wilde may have seen in Terry's Theatre in the late summer of 1894, a now-forgotten play entitled *The Foundling*. Powell describes how that the hero of that play, a young man named Dick Pennell, wishes to marry, but is prevented from doing so by his young lady's formidable maiden aunt and conventional mother on the grounds that he has no family and no proper identity. Like Jack and Algy, he considers a christening as a way of solving his problem; like Jack, he comically identifies the wrong woman as his own mother; and, again like Jack, he asks to know 'who I am' (Act III, p. 311)at the end of the play. Powell argues that the play with food and drink in *Earnest* is derived from several contemporary plays, including Brandon Thomas's farce, *Charley's Aunt* (1892); and that other plot lines are borrowed from French farces that Oscar Wilde might have seen on his many trips abroad. He concludes that the play both borrows from tradition and helps thereby to found a new tradition which combines the genres of farce, comedy of manners and social satire.

The importance of Oscar Wilde's *The Importance of Being Earnest* very possibly resides precisely in it use and adaptation of well-worn theatrical models. For the original audiences there was both the comfort of recognition, and a small shock of the new as the stock figures from farce and comedy gained a new level of inconsequential absurdity in Oscar Wilde's manipulation of them.

World events	Oscar Wilde's life	Literary events
		1674 William Wycherley, *The Country Wife*
		1676 William Wycherley, *The Plain Dealer*
		1696 John Vanbrugh, *The Relapse*
		1700 William Congreve, *The Way of the World*
		1762 Jean Jacques Rousseau, *The Social Contract*
		1773 Oliver Goldsmith, *She Stoops to Conquer*
		1777 Richard Brinsley Sheridan, *The School for Scandal*
1789 Outbreak of French Revolution		**1792** Mary Wollstonecraft, *A Vindication of the Rights of Women*
1793 France declares war on Britain		
1800 Pitt passes bill for the union of Great Britain and Ireland		
1813 Napoleon defeated		
1815 Napoleon escapes from Elba but is defeated at Waterloo		
1832 Reform Bill passed		
1837 Accession of Queen Victoria		
		1841 *Punch, or the London Charivari* started

World events	Oscar Wilde's life	Literary events
1845 Famine in Ireland		
		1847 Charlotte Brontë, *Jane Eyre*; Anne Brontë, *Agnes Grey*; Emily Brontë, *Wuthering Heights*; William Makepeace Thackeray, *Vanity Fair*
1848 Revolutions in Paris; armed rebellion in Ireland fails		**1848** Karl Marx and Frederich Engels, *The Communist Manifesto*
1849 Bedford College for Women founded in London		
1851 Great Exhibition held at Crystal Palace		
	1854 Born in Dublin	**1854** Charles Dickens, *Hard Times*
1857 Indian Mutiny		**1857** Anthony Trollope, *Barchester Towers*
		1860 George Eliot, *The Mill on the Floss*
1861 Beginning of American Civil War		**1861** Charles Dickens, *Great Expectations*
		1863 John Stuart Mill, *Utilitarianism*
		1865 Charles Dickens, *Our Mutual Friend*
		1866 Algernon Charles Swinburne, *Poems and Ballads*
1867 Second Reform Bill; Fenian rising in Ireland		
1868 Gladstone becomes Liberal Prime Minister		

CHRONOLOGY

World events	Oscar Wilde's life	Literary events
1870 Gladstone passes First Irish Land Act; First Married Women's Property Act		
1871 Paris Commune suppressed; in Britain Trade Union Act gives unions legal status		**1871** John Ruskin, *Fors Clavigera*
		1873 Walter Pater, *Studies in the History of the Renaissance*
1874 Disraeli becomes Conservative Prime Minister	**1874** Moves to Oxford	**1874** First Impressionist Exhibition in Paris; Thomas Hardy, *Far From the Madding Crowd*
		1875 Anthony Trollope, *The Way We Live Now*
	1876 His father, Sir William Wilde, dies	
	1878 Leaves Oxford having won Newdigate Prize for Poetry	**1878** William Gilbert and Arthur Sullivan, *HMS Pinafore*
		1879 Henrik Ibsen, *A Doll's House*
1880 Gladstone becomes Prime Minister again; civil disturbances in Ireland		
1881 Gladstone passes Second Irish Land Act	**1881** *Poems* is published	**1881** William Gilbert and Arthur Sullivan, *Patience*; Henrik Ibsen, *Ghosts*; Arthur Wing Pinero, *The Money Spinner*
1882 Second Married Women's Property Act	**1882** Goes on lecture tour of USA; *Vera or the Nihilists*	
1883 Irish terrorist bombings in London		

CHRONOLOGY

World events	Oscar Wilde's life	Literary events
1884 Third Reform Act	**1884** Marries Constance Lloyd	
1885 The Labouchère Amendment to the Criminal Law Act makes homosexual acts in private a crime	**1885** His son, Cyril, is born	**1885** William Gilbert and Arthur Sullivan, *The Mikado*
1886 Gladstone prepares Home Rule Bill for Ireland but is defeated and resigns	**1886** His son, Vyvyan, is born; meets Robert Ross; becomes involved in a series of illicit homosexual affairs	**1886** Robert Louis Stevenson, *The Strange Case of Dr Jekyll and Mr Hyde*
	1887 Becomes editor of *The Lady's World*	**1887** Rudyard Kipling, *Plain Tales from the Hills*
	1888 *The Happy Prince and Other Stories*	
	1891 *A House of Pomegranates; Lord Arthur Savile's Crime; Intentions*; 'The Soul of Man Under Socialism'; *Salomé* is written; *The Picture of Dorian Gray*	**1891** Thomas Hardy, *Tess of the D'Urbervilles*
1892 Gladstone returns to office as Prime Minister; Keir Hardie founds the Independent Labour Party	**1892** *Lady Windermere's Fan* first performed; first meets and falls in love with Lord Alfred Douglas	**1892** Brandon Thomas, *Charley's Aunt*; George Bernard Shaw, *Widowers' Houses*
	1893 *A Woman of No Importance* first performed	**1893** Ernest Christopher Dowson (with Arthur Collin Moore), *A Comedy of Masks*; William Butler Yeats, *The Lake Isle of Innisfree*
1894 Sarah Grand coins term New Woman	**1894** 'The Sphinx'; *Salomé* is published	**1894** Rudyard Kipling, *The Jungle Book*

World events	Oscar Wilde's life	Literary events
	1895 *An Ideal Husband* first performed; *The Importance of Being Earnest* first staged; sues the Marquis of Queensbury – Lord Douglas's father; sentenced to two years hard labour in prison	**1895** Thomas Hardy, *Jude the Obscure*; H.G. Wells, *The Time Machine*
	1897 Released from prison and moves to France; uses the pseudonym Sebastian Melmoth	**1897** Max Beerbohm, *The Happy Hypocrite*
	1898 *The Ballad of Reading Gaol* is published anonymously	**1898** H.G. Wells, *The War of the Worlds*
	1900 Converts to Roman Catholicism; dies in Paris of meningitis on November 30	
1901 Death of Queen Victoria		**1901** Rudyard Kipling, *Kim*
		1902 William Butler Yeats, *Cathleen ni Hoolihan*
1903 Women's Social and Political Union founded to demand votes for women		**1903** George Bernard Shaw, *Man and Superman*
		1904 Joseph Conrad, *Nostromo*
	1905 *De Profundis* is published (partly)	
1906 Liberals achieve big victory in General Election and gain support of Irish Nationalists		**1906** John Galsworthy, *A Man of Property*
		1907 Joseph Conrad, *The Secret Agent*

World events	Oscar Wilde's life	Literary events
1908 Asquith becomes Liberal Prime Minister; Votes for Women march in Hyde Park		
		1910 H.G. Wells, *The History of Mr Polly*
		1913 George Bernard Shaw, *Androcles and the Lion*; D.H. Lawrence, *Sons and Lovers*
1914-18 First World War		**1914** James Joyce, *Dubliners*
		1920 John Galsworthy, *Awakening*
		1922 James Joyce, *Ulysses*
		1924 E.M. Forster, *A Passage to India*
		1928 D.H. Lawrence, *Lady Chatterley's Lover*
1939-45 Second World War		**1939** James Joyce, *Finnegans Wake*
		1941 Noel Coward, *Blithe Spirit*
		1945 Evelyn Waugh, *Brideshead revisited*; George Orwell, *Animal Farm*
1957 The Wolfenden Report supports the repeal of anti-homosexual legislation		
	1962 *De Profundis* is published in full	
1967 The Labouchère Amendment is repealed, legalising homosexual relationships for consenting males over 21 years old		

LITERARY TERMS

aesthetic movement an unofficial and loosely based European movement in the arts, including literature, flourishing the second half of the nineteenth century, which stressed the paramount value and self-sufficiency of art. The catch-phrase of the movement was 'Art for Art's sake'. The ideas of aestheticism originated in France, but they found their way to Britain through writers like Algernon Charles Swinburne, Walter Pater, Oscar Wilde, Ernest Dowson, Lionel Johnson and Arthur Symons. In their writings, art is viewed as the supreme human achievement. It should never become subservient to moral, political, didactic or practical purposes. Art exists merely for the sake of its own beauty and it can be judged only by its own criteria

ambiguity (noun), **ambiguous** (adjective) [from the Latin for 'doubtful, shifting'] the capacity of words and sentences to have double, multiple or uncertain meanings. A pun is the simplest form of ambiguity, where a single word is used with two sharply different meanings, usually for comic effect. Ambiguity may also arise from syntax (when it is difficult to disentangle the grammar of a sentence to resolve a single meaning), and from tone (where the reader cannot tell, for example, whether a given text is to be read seriously or not)

apron stage a stage which juts out into the audience. An apron stage is usually four-sided, with three of the four sides surrounded by the audience, and the fourth side made up of a back drop or the theatre's back wall. It is seldom a regular rectangle or square, but has converging sides, making it look from above like the basic shape of a kitchen apron

avant garde [from the French for 'before the guard' or vanguard] originally a military expression to describe the foremost part of an army, the word is now commonly used to describe modern artists and writers whose works are (or were) deliberately and self-consciously experimental, who set out to discover new forms, techniques and subject matter in the arts

binary opposition the fundamental contrasts (such as in/out, off/on, good/bad, cops/robbers) used in structuralist methods of analysis and literary criticism. Literature can be interpreted through frameworks of oppositions of this kind. Indeed, it has been argued that binarism is fundamental to all learning and interpretation of experience, and that all processes of understanding involve a discrimination and choice between opposed possibilities. If we ask ourselves whether an action is good, this is only comprehensible in terms of its opposite, bad. 'Up' and 'down' are relative terms, not absolutes: they only have meaning in relation to each other. More recently critics have started to focus on the idea that binary oppositions have fixed values in relation to each other, and that one term on any opposition is always seen as relatively positive in relation to the other. Structuralist, feminist, gay and post-structuralist critics are therefore often interested in seeing the places in which these traditional values are overturned

camp a word of uncertain derivation, camp refers to an attitude – to life, and to the arts – which is ironic, stylised and distanced, and which overturns the traditional values of binary oppositions. It relies on comically exaggerated responses to inappropriate subjects. Such an attitude has often been associated with gay writers and performers, but it is not necessarily a homosexual phenomenon

comedy of manners a sub-division of comedy. Comedy is used most often to describe a kind of drama which is intended primarily to entertain its audience, and which ends happily for the characters with whom the audience sympathises. The comedy of manners, which developed during the Restoration period, focuses on the love intrigues of cynical and sophisticated young aristocrats in high society: it relies heavily on verbal wit rather than on elements of slapstick or farce. Comedy of manners often upends conventional expectations by rewarding unscrupulous but clever characters

dénouement [from the French for 'unknotting, untying'] the final unfolding of the plot

drag refers to a theatrical tradition in which men play women's parts dressed up in costume. The pantomime dame is one example of the drag artiste. More recently, drag has also become a popular kind of cabaret act

dramatic irony dramatic irony occurs when the development of the plot allows the audience to possess more information about what is happening than the characters. The effect of this can be either comic or tragic

euphemism [from the Greek for 'speaking fair'] unpleasant, embarrassing or frightening facts or words can be concealed behind a euphemism: a word or phrase that is less blunt, rude or frightening than a direct naming of the fact or word might be. Hence 'to kick the bucket' is a euphemism for death; 'would you like to wash you hands?' is a polite euphemism for the question 'would you like to urinate?' Sexual functions, death and body parts are typically disguised in this way in common speech

farce [from the French for 'stuffing'] a kind of drama intended primarily to provoke laughter, using exaggerated characters and complicated plots, full of absurd episodes, ludicrous situations and knockabout action. Mistaken identity is often a element in the plot. **Bedroom farce** concentrates on marital infidelity and sexual escapades: the typical stage setting involves a large number of doors through which characters enter and exit at moments inconvenient to each other. Unlike satire, farce has no moral purpose, and is not censorious

genre [from the French for 'type, kind'] the term for a type or kind of literature, referring first to the major divisions of writing – drama, prose, poetry – then to subdivisions within the larger categories. A drama, for example, might be a tragedy or a comedy; a comedy might be a comedy of manners, a farce, a romantic comedy or social satire. The importance of genre is that it gives readers/viewers an horizon of expectation, a set of criteria against which to judge the piece before them. Farce that does not make its audience laugh is not fulfilling its generic function

homophobic (adjective), **homophobia** (noun) this is a relatively recent coinage. It describes an attitude which is violently antipathetic to gay men and lesbians, an attitude which may be found in individual responses, but which also is seen to affect entire cultures and their institutions such as the legal and education systems and the religious establishment

hyperbole [from the Greek for 'throwing too far'] emphasis by exaggeration

ingenu(e) [from the French for 'ingenuous, innocent] the ingenue is a stock character from the comedy of manners. Usually female, often from the country (in contrast with the urban sophistication of the majority of the characters), she is innocent, naïve, artless and easily manipulated

in the round describes a performing space which is entirely surrounded by the audience. The spectator is generally much closer to the action on the stage than would be the case with a proscenium arch theatre. Playing in the round therefore gives the audience a much more intimate experience of any play

irony [from the Greek for 'dissembling'] irony consists of saying one thing when you mean another. Irony is achieved through understatement, concealment and allusion, rather than by direct statement

melodrama [from the Greek for 'sung drama'] melodrama was an important theatrical genre in nineteenth-century theatre. Originally it meant a play with music. In the nineteenth century many theatres put on plays with musical accompaniment as a way of evading the licensing laws which required serious drama to be passed for performance by the Lord Chamberlain's office. These plays were naïvely sensational, with simple, flat characterisation, unrelentingly vicious villains plotting to trap virtuous maidens, and much bloodthirsty action. They were fast-paced entertainment aimed at a mass audience, and were very popular for most of the Victorian age

modernism (noun), **modernist** (adjective) modernism is the label which describes some of the characteristics of some twentieth-century avant garde writing, often thought to have been developed in hostile reaction both to the conventions of nineteenth-century realism and to the conditions of modern life. Its most typical feature is its experimental qualities, in particular in new forms and subjects for art and literature. Modernist writers also generally rejected nineteenth-century critical concerns with morality, didacticism and political purpose

moral a lesson that can be extracted from a story, play or fable. The moral is often related to poetic justice, in which, as Miss Prism might say, the good end happily and the bad end unhappily

motif a motif is some aspect of literature (for example, a kind of character, a particular theme or image) which recurs frequently

naturalist, naturalistic naturalism is a development from realism. In novels it refers to a pessimistic world-view in which characters can never be free from their fates in which biology and social position combine to make them what they are. In the theatre, however, naturalism refers to the conventions by which the theatre of the late nineteenth century and beyond tried to maintain the illusion of complete reality on the stage. The plots of naturalist plays were set in contemporary society; the action was supposed to be entirely probable and believable. Settings and costumes were very exact. And the playing style of the actors was as realistic as possible, with no overtly theatrical gestures and no direct addresses to the audience. The aim was to make the audience forget that what they were seeing was merely a theatrical spectacle, and to get them to believe utterly in the world on the stage

neologism [from the Greek for 'new word'] an innovation in language, an invented or newly coined word. Although new words enter the English language all the time, traditionalists often view neologism as a bad thing

new drama the phrase describes a movement in drama from the end of the nineteenth century. It was a reaction against the melodramas of popular theatre, and moved towards the idea that drama should be intellectually challenging and stimulating, that it should deal with difficult and previously uncovered topics, and that the audience should be made to think as well as to enjoy itself. It was, however, a minority interest at the time when Oscar Wilde was writing

New Woman a term coined in 1894 to describe a woman who went against late-Victorian views about proper femininity, who agitated for better women's rights, who sought a university education, a career and the vote. The 'New Woman' was seen by her admirers as an intelligent, interesting and exciting development in contrast to the enfeebled 'lady' who was the ideal of the traditionalists. The 'New Woman' was also attacked widely in the press for her free and easy manners, her refusal to be chaperoned, her intellectual ambition and even her clothes. Hostile critics saw her as an ugly bluestocking who had lost all her femininity paradox [from the Greek for 'beside-opinion'] an apparently self-contradictory statement, or a statement that seems in conflict with logic or opinion. Lying behind this superficial absurdity, however, is a meaning or a truth

periphrasis (noun), periphrastic (adjective) [from the Greek for 'speaking around'] an indirect manner of speech, often used for comic purposes

phatic language [from the Greek for 'utterance'] words and phrases used in social situations to establish a relationship between the speakers. Jack's 'Charming day it has been, Miss Fairfax' (p. 263) has no communicative function except to begin the conversation. In itself, a phatic phrase has almost no meaning; but it is an important and significant way of opening communication between people

problem play a play which examines a sociological problem. The term was current to describe plays in the late nineteenth century, when the 'problem' when the problem was always the issue of female sexuality – extramarital sex and pregnancy, adultery and divorce

proscenium arch [from the Greek for 'in front of the scene'] in the traditional theatre, the proscenium arch is the space filled by the curtain. A small portion of the stage may jut out beyond the arch, but the majority of the stage space lies behind it. This is the traditional stage for nineteenth- and early twentieth-century drama: it looks like a room with one of its walls missing. The audience sits at some distance from action in most cases because of the orchestra pit which lies between the stage and the seating

realism the word has many applications, but broadly speaking it refers to the tendency in literature to portray the real world without softening its appearance (as idealist kinds of writing would tend to do); realism aims to tell the unglossed truth about reality. It refers to a set of conventions by which the real might be expressed rather than to reality itself. Realism was the dominant mode of nineteenth-century fiction, but its application is often misleading to students because of the subjects that realism could not consider in the context of a conservative audience. The reality realism portrayed was often very selective

referentiality the key note of a realist text is that it *refers* to reality. Realism therefore is referential

repartee [from the French for 'reply swiftly'] a term derived from fencing, repartee indicates witty, swift replies, often mildly insulting. It is a common conversational mode in the comedy of manners

satire literature which exhibits or examines a vice or a folly and makes it appear ridiculous. Although satire often appears in comic writing, it has a serious purpose, in that it seeks to show that vice it considers is wrong. It uses laughter as a force to attack its subjects, rather than permitting its audience just to laugh for pleasure. **Social satire** uses the weapons of satire to attack a particular society and its moral values. Satire can be used therefore as an instrument of **social critique**, an explicit or implicit criticism of society

semantic [from the Greek for 'significant'] as an adjective, semantic is a near equivalent of 'meaning'. In linguistics, semantics is the study of the meanings of words, of how words express their meanings, and of how meanings change through time

semiotic system a collection of signs, verbal, visual or performative, which have meaning. Semiotics describes the theory that all signs can be interpreted

separate spheres debate from the mid nineteenth century onwards, there was a series of debates in the British press about the proper relationships between men and women. This Victorian version of the battle of the sexes came to be known as the separate spheres debate because of the argument current amongst conservative writers that a woman's sphere was the home and a man's was the public domain. In the view of many contemporary writers, a woman's role was entirely bound up with domesticity and being a good wife and mother; a man's role was to support her by performing his public duties in the world of paid employment. The debate became more polarised as the century progressed and it became clear that many women could not or would not marry, and that they too sought properly remunerated work outside the home

sight gag a visual (as opposed to a verbal) joke.

solecism [from the Greek for 'using incorrect syntax'] a solecism is a verbal intervention which breaks the rules of normal or polite grammar. By extension, it can also refer to an impolite or inappropriate action

stage business non-verbal action that takes place on the stage. This can either be explicitly scripted in stage directions (as in *Earnest* Act I, where Oscar Wilde has scripted a slapstick routine around Jack's cigarette case); or it can be action instigated by a directing or acting decision

stock character the kind of character particularly associated with a particular genre. The stock characters of the comedy of manners, for example, might include a dissolute young rake, a young female ingenue, a comically ineffectual elderly lady, or the older female battle-axe

structuralism structuralism proceeds from the idea that words have no natural relationship with their meanings. Instead, words and their meanings are connected only arbitrarily and conventionally. We understand language by being well-versed in its conventions, and by its structures of difference: 'cat' is different from 'hat' or 'can'. By extentions, structural theorists have argued that all meaning is structured by difference and convention – from individual sentences to entire genres, from pictures to performances. The reader/spectator knows the 'rules' of structure, and notices when performances or language practices depart from the rules. Its importance in literary criticism is that it disrupts the idea that language is directly expressive of the individual author's sincere emotional state. Rather writers and their characters are instances of role-playing, performances of arbitrary rules which are more or less conventional

suspense the condition of wanting desperately to know what happens next in a narrative or dramatic plot

well-made play a play which exhibits a neatness of plot and smooth-functioning exactness of action, with all its parts fitting together. A well-made play leaves no loose ends and its audience knows exactly what to think at the end

Ruth Robbins is Senior Lecturer in English at Leeds Metropolitan University. She has written a number of essays on Oscar Wilde and the late nineteenth century, and is author of *Literary Feminisms* (Palgrave Macmillan, 2000) and *Pater to Forster, 1873-1924* (Palgrave Macmillan, 2003). She is currently completing a book on *Subjectivity*.

General Editor
Martin Gray, former Head of the Department of English Studies at the University of Stirling, and Literary Studies at the University of Luton.

Maya Angelou
I Know Why the Caged Bird Sings

Jane Austen
Pride and Prejudice

Alan Ayckbourn
Absent Friends

Elizabeth Barrett Browning
Selected Poems

Robert Bolt
A Man for All Seasons

Harold Brighouse
Hobson's Choice

Charlotte Brontë
Jane Eyre

Emily Brontë
Wuthering Heights

Shelagh Delaney
A Taste of Honey

Charles Dickens
David Copperfield
Great Expectations
Hard Times
Oliver Twist

Roddy Doyle
Paddy Clarke Ha Ha Ha

George Eliot
Silas Marner
The Mill on the Floss

Anne Frank
The Diary of a Young Girl

William Golding
Lord of the Flies

Oliver Goldsmith
She Stoops to Conquer

Willis Hall
The Long and the Short and the Tall

Thomas Hardy
Far from the Madding Crowd
The Mayor of Casterbridge
Tess of the d'Urbervilles
The Withered Arm and other Wessex Tales

L.P. Hartley
The Go-Between

Seamus Heaney
Selected Poems

Susan Hill
I'm the King of the Castle

Barry Hines
A Kestrel for a Knave

Louise Lawrence
Children of the Dust

Harper Lee
To Kill a Mockingbird

Laurie Lee
Cider with Rosie

Arthur Miller
The Crucible
A View from the Bridge

Robert O'Brien
Z for Zachariah

Frank O'Connor
My Oedipus Complex and Other Stories

George Orwell
Animal Farm

J.B. Priestley
An Inspector Calls
When We Are Married

Willy Russell
Educating Rita
Our Day Out

J.D. Salinger
The Catcher in the Rye

William Shakespeare
Henry IV Part I
Henry V
Julius Caesar
Macbeth
The Merchant of Venice
A Midsummer Night's Dream
Much Ado About Nothing
Romeo and Juliet
The Tempest
Twelfth Night

George Bernard Shaw
Pygmalion

Mary Shelley
Frankenstein

R.C. Sherriff
Journey's End

Rukshana Smith
Salt on the snow

John Steinbeck
Of Mice and Men

Robert Louis Stevenson
Dr Jekyll and Mr Hyde

Jonathan Swift
Gulliver's Travels

Robert Swindells
Daz 4 Zoe

Mildred D. Taylor
Roll of Thunder, Hear My Cry

Mark Twain
Huckleberry Finn

James Watson
Talking in Whispers

Edith Wharton
Ethan Frome

William Wordsworth
Selected Poems

A Choice of Poets

Mystery Stories of the Nineteenth Century including The Signalman

Nineteenth Century Short Stories

Poetry of the First World War

Six Women Poets

For the AQA Anthology:

Duffy and Armitage & Pre-1914 Poetry

Heaney and Clarke & Pre-1914 Poetry

Poems from Different Cultures

Margaret Atwood
Cat's Eye
The Handmaid's Tale

Jane Austen
Emma
Mansfield Park
Persuasion
Pride and Prejudice
Sense and Sensibility

Alan Bennett
Talking Heads

William Blake
Songs of Innocence and of Experience

Charlotte Brontë
Jane Eyre
Villette

Emily Brontë
Wuthering Heights

Angela Carter
Nights at the Circus

Geoffrey Chaucer
The Franklin's Prologue and Tale
The Merchant's Prologue and Tale
The Miller's Prologue and Tale
The Prologue to the Canterbury Tales
The Wife of Bath's Prologue and Tale

Samuel Coleridge
Selected Poems

Joseph Conrad
Heart of Darkness

Daniel Defoe
Moll Flanders

Charles Dickens
Bleak House
Great Expectations
Hard Times

Emily Dickinson
Selected Poems

John Donne
Selected Poems

Carol Ann Duffy
Selected Poems

George Eliot
Middlemarch
The Mill on the Floss

T.S. Eliot
Selected Poems
The Waste Land

F. Scott Fitzgerald
The Great Gatsby

E.M. Forster
A Passage to India

Brian Friel
Translations

Thomas Hardy
Jude the Obscure
The Mayor of Casterbridge
The Return of the Native
Selected Poems
Tess of the d'Urbervilles

Seamus Heaney
Selected Poems from 'Opened Ground'

Nathaniel Hawthorne
The Scarlet Letter

Homer
The Iliad
The Odyssey

Aldous Huxley
Brave New World

Kazuo Ishiguro
The Remains of the Day

Ben Jonson
The Alchemist

James Joyce
Dubliners

John Keats
Selected Poems

Philip Larkin
The Whitsun Weddings and Selected Poems

Christopher Marlowe
Doctor Faustus
Edward II

Arthur Miller
Death of a Salesman

John Milton
Paradise Lost Books I & II

Toni Morrison
Beloved

George Orwell
Nineteen Eighty-Four

Sylvia Plath
Selected Poems

Alexander Pope
Rape of the Lock & Selected Poems

William Shakespeare
Antony and Cleopatra
As You Like It
Hamlet
Henry IV Part I
King Lear
Macbeth
Measure for Measure
The Merchant of Venice
A Midsummer Night's Dream
Much Ado About Nothing
Othello
Richard II
Richard III
Romeo and Juliet
The Taming of the Shrew
The Tempest
Twelfth Night
The Winter's Tale

George Bernard Shaw
Saint Joan

Mary Shelley
Frankenstein

Jonathan Swift
Gulliver's Travels and A Modest Proposal

Alfred Tennyson
Selected Poems

Virgil
The Aeneid

Alice Walker
The Color Purple

Oscar Wilde
The Importance of Being Earnest

Tennessee Williams
A Streetcar Named Desire
The Glass Menagerie

Jeanette Winterson
Oranges Are Not the Only Fruit

John Webster
The Duchess of Malfi

Virginia Woolf
To the Lighthouse

William Wordsworth
The Prelude and Selected Poems

W.B. Yeats
Selected Poems

Metaphysical Poets